Florian Aicher
Ibrahim Altindal
Bernardo Bader
Josef Bär
Markus Baurenhas
Ewald Bechter
Alexander Bechter
Dietmar Bechter
Hermann Bechter
Florian Bechter
Christoph Bechter
Michael Beer
Mario Beer
Adolf Bereuter
Nadja Berkmann
Benjamin Bilgeri
Johannes Böhler
Mark Bösch
Renate Breuss
Frank Broger
Margarete Broger
Günter Bucher
Hassan Cinar
Dieter Dorner
Wolfgang Dorner
Johannes Dünser
Guntram Düringer
Josef Eberle (Bildstein)
Josef Eberle (Hittisau)
Ronny Engelhard
Michael Esins
Ulrich Faistenauer
Georg Faschin
Elmar Felder
Albert Felizeter
Michael Fetz
Hubert Feuerstein
Robert Feuerstein
Walter Feurstein
Nadezda Filipovic
Manfred Fink
Wolfgang Fink
Peter Fink
Dominik Fischer
Markus Flatz
Josef Fröwis
Benjamin Fröwis
Patrick Fröwis
Martin Fuchs
Karlheinz Gasser
Ingo Gehrer
Manuela Grissemann
Marcel Haltmeier
Reinhard Haltmeyer
Norman Hambach
Wilhelmine Hangler
Michael Harrer
Manuela Heschl
Patrick Hiller
Johanna Hiller
Andreas Hirschbühl
Manfred Immler
Annegret Ischepp
Michael Kaufmann
Karin Kaufmann
Anton Kaufmann
Tugba Kaya
Stefan Kleber
Michael Knapp
Arno Kohler
Vlado Kovacevic
Arno Kraxner
Stefan Künzler
Wolfgang Lässer
Martin Lässer
Theodor Lehner
Bertram Lenz
Sandro Lerch
Michael Loitz
Michael Loughridge
Josef Manser
Otto Manser
Sven Matt
Andreas Mätzler
Gotthard Maurer
Max Metzler
Thomas Metzler

werkraum krone

Vom Neuen Handwerk und dem Umbau eines
alteingesessenen Gasthofs im Bregenzerwald

A tale of new and old – outstanding craftmanship and
the rebuild of a traditional Bregenzerwald coaching inn

BUCHER

BUCHER Verlag Hohenems
www.bucherverlag.com

© werkraum bregenzerwald, Egg & Gasthof Krone, Hittisau
1. Auflage, Mai 2008
1st edition May 2008

Herausgeber Published by	werkraum bregenzerwald, Egg
	Gasthof Krone, Hittisau
Autoren Text	Florian Aicher, Rotis
	Renate Breuss, Rankweil
	Peter Natter, Hittisau
Gestaltung Layout	Frank Broger, Andelsbuch
Lektorat Editing	Peter Natter, Hittisau
Übersetzung Translation	Michael Loughridge, Scotland, UK
	Angelika Muir-Hartmann, Scotland, UK
Fotografie Photos	Adolf Bereuter, Lauterach
Planskizzen Architect's drawings	Bernardo Bader, Dornbirn
Projektleitung Project Manager	Isabella Natter-Spets, Bregenz
Druck und Verlag Printing and publishers	BUCHER Druck Verlag Netzwerk, Hohenems

Printed in Austria
ISBN 978-3-902612-67-0

Gemeinsam Schaffen Creatively together	4
Land und Leute The country and the people	10
Früher war gestern … Once upon a time was only yesterday …	12
Die Krone in Hittisau The Krone at Hittisau	18
Miteinander von Alt und Neu Old and New in harmony	22
Krone-Umbau Krone Alterations	28
Unsichtbare Kräfte Unsichtbare Kräfte	30
werkraum The werkraum	34
Werkstätten Craft workshops	48
Streng und Locker Strict yet easy-going	66
Vertraut und neu The familiar and the new	68
Für sich und gemeinsam On one's own and together	74
Kochen und Bauen Cooks too are builders	82
Baustelle Küche The kitchen as building site	84
Handwerker zu Tisch Craftworkers' lunch	86
Rohstoff Landschaft Raw materials: countryside	90
Familiäre Prägung A family thing	94
Ästhetik der Sparsamkeit Good taste and restraint	96
Der Gast in der Krone The guest experience at the Krone	98
Die Mitwirkenden The participants	112
werkraum bregenzerwald werkraum bregenzerwald	114
Gasthof Krone Gasthof Krone	114
Schlusswort A final reflection	116
Die Autoren The authors	118

Gemeinsam Schaffen

Wir leben sehr gerne im Bregenzerwald. Nicht nur, weil seine Landschaft mit den sanften Hügeln, satten Feldern, den Tobeln und schroffen Hängen ein ganz besonderes Stück Landschaft ist. Sondern auch deswegen, weil man hier eine spezielle Atmosphäre spürt: an der Schlichtheit und Geradlinigkeit von Häusern und Räumen, dem gelebten Brauchtum in friedlicher Koexistenz mit der Offenheit Neuem gegenüber, dem Stolz der Leute und einem lebendigen Gemeinwesen – einer starken regionalen Identität also, die wohl geschichtlich begründet ist und sich bis heute hält.

Wenn man in einer solchen Region lebt, möchte man sein Umfeld nicht nur nutzen. Es ist uns Anliegen, daran mitzuwirken, dass der Bregenzerwald lebenswert ist. Daher beziehen wir viele Produkte von Landwirten aus dem „Wald". Als es daran ging, Teile unseres Gasthofs umzubauen, war klar, daß Architekt und Handwerker, sowie ein Großteil des verwendeten Materials aus der Region kommen werden. Dieser erste Entschluß mündete in eine fruchtbare Zusammenarbeit mit dem werkraum bregenzerwald – der Plattform für das Neue Handwerk im Bregenzerwald. Die Mitarbeiter von 13 werkraum-Mitgliedsbetrieben arbeiteten in der Krone Hand in Hand, brachten in Gesprächen wertvolle Anregungen, neue Lösungen und eigene Ideen ein und ließen in knapp zwei Monaten einen neuen Eingangsbereich, zwei neue Stuben und sechs geräumige Gästezimmer entstehen. Hier ist die für den Bregenzerwald typische hohe Handwerksqualität und geradlinige Formensprache zu erleben. Und vielleicht läßt sich sogar etwas von dem Geist erahnen, der uns alle angetrieben hat: für jene, die im Gasthof Krone einkehren, etwas ganz Besonderes entstehen zu lassen. Dieses Buch dokumentiert das gemeinsame Schaffen der werkraum-Betriebe in unserem Haus, es portraitiert die Entwicklung des Gasthof Krone vom Gestern zum Heute und vielleicht bietet es Ihnen auch Inspirationen, wenn es darum geht, Wohlfühlräume jenseits der standardisierten Industrieware zu gestalten.

Helene und Dietmar Nussbaumer
Gasthof Krone

Trends und Design kommen gemäss landläufiger Meinung meistens aus den Großstädten und Ballungsräumen. Es kann auch umgekehrt sein. Seit knapp 10 Jahren agiert im Bregenzerwald eine Initiative von modernen Handwerksbetrieben, die ihren Sitz alle auf dem Land haben und viele Architekten und Designer aus der Stadt in den Bregenzerwald locken: der werkraum bregenzerwald. Der werkraum bregenzerwald ist der Zusammenschluss von aktuell 93 Handwerks- und Gewerbebetrieben mit Marktanteilen im In- und Ausland. Kerngeschäft ist die Förderung und Verbindung von Handwerk und Design, von neuesten Technologien und bewährten Handwerkstechniken. In unseren Aktivitäten, in den Wettbewerben, Ausstellungen und Nachwuchsprojekten arbeiten Meister und Lehrlinge aus unterschiedlichsten Branchen zusammen, entwickeln gemeinsam mit Architekten und Gestaltern ihre Produkte, bilden ihre Netzwerke. In der täglichen Arbeit spielen diese betriebs- und branchenübergreifenden Kooperationen eine immer größere Rolle, die Stärkung und Forcierung solcher Projekte ist dem werkraum ein wichtiges Anliegen.

Mit dem Kronenprojekt in Hittisau ist eine neue Kooperationsform entstanden. Die Ausstattung von Gasthöfen und Hotels durch Bregenzerwälder Handwerker ist an sich nichts Neues. Neu ist das klare Bekenntnis zu unserer Arbeit und zur Region, die Verknüpfung von anspruchsvoller Gastronomie mit ebenso anspruchsvollem Handwerk und die Darstellung und Veröffentlichung in dieser Dokumentation.

Die Sanierung und der Umbau des Gasthofs Krone vermittelt nicht nur am anschaulichen Beispiel, sondern auch über dieses Buch, wie das Handwerk im Bregenzerwald lebt, wie das Zusammenspiel von Branchen und Gestaltern funktioniert, von wo wir alle herkommen und wohin die Reise gehen kann. Als Mitherausgeber und Obmann möchte ich allen, die bei diesem geglückten Projekt ihre Hand im Spiel hatten, herzlich danken. Ganz speziell aber den Bauherren Helene und Dietmar Nussbaumer, ihnen möchten wir viel Erfolg und Freude mit der neuen Krone wünschen.

Anton Kaufmann
Obmann werkraum bregenzerwald

We love it here in the Bregenzerwald. Not just because our landscape, with its gentle hills and rich pastures, its ravines and steep slopes, makes this an outstanding bit of countryside – there is something more, a special atmosphere which one senses in the simple forms and straight lines of houses, spaces and rooms, in the traditional way of life that manages to coexist peacefully with open-mindedness to the new; in the proud independence of the people and the vigour of the community life; in short, in a strong regional identity that surely reaches far back in time and still flourishes today.

Living in a region like this, one feels it is not enough to simply use our surroundings as a resource. We aim to help ensure that the Bregenzerwald is a good place to live in. That's why we buy many of our supplies from farmers here in the "Wald". And when we decided to rebuild parts of our hotel, it was clear in our minds that the architect and the workpeople, and a large part of the materials used, would be local. This initial decision led to our fruitful collaboration with werkraum bregenzerwald – the organisation representing New Crafts in the Bregenzerwald region. Craftworkers from 13 firms affiliated to the werkraum worked hand-in-glove with each other on the Krone rebuild, their discussions with each other bringing mutual stimulation, fresh solutions and original ideas – and in just under two months they had built a new entrance and foyer, two new Stuben to eat and drink in, and six spacious new hotel rooms. Here our guests can appreciate the Bregenzerwald region's quality craftsmanship and characteristic design preference for rectilinear forms. Perhaps they may even gain an inkling of the spirit that inspired us all – our resolve that visitors to the Krone in future would encounter something really special. This book is a record of the creative work shared at our hotel by the werkraum businesses, tells the story of the Gasthof Krone from long ago up to the present day, and it may even be the inspiration you need if you yourself are seeking to design rooms that will give a sense of wellbeing – and if you need quality and individuality rather than standardised units.

Helene and Dietmar Nussbaumer
of the Gasthof Krone

Creatively together

Trendiness and new designs are widely held to emanate from the great cities and conurbations. But the reality can be quite different. For just on 10 years now, the Bregenzerwald has been home to an initiative made up of modern craft businesses, all of them rural-based, that are attracting numbers of architects and designers to leave the cities for the Bregenzerwald. The group is called werkraum bregenzerwald. This werkraum is an alliance of – currently – 93 handcraft and general businesses catering to domestic and foreign markets. The core activity is the promotion and synergising of hand crafts and design, very latest technology and proven handicraft skills. In our various activities, in the competitions, exhibitions and training-linked projects, the pattern is for masters and apprentices from a huge variety of trades to collaborate with each other, develop their products through consultation with architects and designers, and build their networks. Cooperation on these lines between different firms and between specialisms has a steadily growing role in day-to-day work, and the werkraum sees it as important to strengthen and promote this type of project.

The Gasthof Krone project at Hittisau is the start of a new form of cooperation. Of course there is nothing new as such in the Bregenzerwald's inns and hotels being fitted and furnished by local craftsmen. The new features are the explicit dedication made to our work and our home region, the association created between fine cuisine and fine handcraft work, and the fact that the project was documented for publication in book form.

Modernised and rebuilt as it is today, the Gasthof Krone is a vivid example – both in its physical presence and through the medium of this book – of how craft skills live on in the Bregenzerwald, of how the reciprocity between different trades and different designers functions in practice, and of where we may be headed. As joint editor and as project director I should like here to express my sincere thanks to everyone involved in the success of this project – and most of all to our clients, Helene and Dietmar Nussbaumer. We wish them every success and many happy years running the new Krone.

Anton Kaufmann
Chairman, werkraum bregenzerwald

Die Kronenfamilie und der Großteil der am Umbau beteiligten HandwerkerInnen präsentieren sich anlässlich eines gemeinsamen Essens im Jänner 2008 dem Fotografen: So ist aus der Arbeit ein Fest geworden.

The Gasthof Krone family and most of the craftsmen and craftswomen who worked on the rebuild pose for the camera. The occasion was the end-of-project feast in January 2008 – the hard work became a celebration.

Land und Leute

Joseph Ritter von Bergmann, 1796 und somit im selben Jahr wie der Erbauer der Krone, Johann Konrad Bechter, geboren, machte als Jurist Karriere in der kaiserlichen Verwaltung. 1831 wurde er als Lehrer zu den Söhnen Erzherzog Karls gerufen. Schließlich ernannte ihn Franz-Joseph I. zum Direktor des Münz- und Antikenkabinetts in Wien. Zur Vollendung des 40. Dienstjahres verlieh ihm der Kaiser den Adelstitel. Mit seiner Heimatgemeinde Hittisau verband den Gelehrten eine innige Beziehung. Von einem seiner letzten Besuche, diesmal in Gesellschaft des großen Mozart-Forschers Ritter von Köchel, schreibt Bergmann am 13. August 1865 an seine Frau in Wien:

„Abends am Dienstag, den 8ten, kamen wir in Hittisau in dem aufs beste eingerichteten Gasthaus zur Krone, bei Bechters an, wo wir Speis, Zimmer, Betten von höchster Qualität fanden und noch finden ... Es gefällt ihm (d.i. Ritter von Köchel) hier überaus wohl, er besuchte meine Brüder mit mir, macht täglich die kleinen Wanderungen mit und ist mit der Lieblichkeit, dem Reize der Landschaft, mit Bechters Haus (also mit der Krone), kurz mit Land und Leuten durchaus zufrieden und fühlt sich bei diesen sehr schönen Tagen in dem stillen Tale (...) so behaglich, dass weder er noch wir so bald wegzugehen gedenken."

Zitiert nach Dr. Anton Stöckler, Hittisau
Quote after Dr. Anton Stöckler, Hittisau

The country and the people

Joseph Ritter von Bergmann, born in 1796 – like Johann Konrad Bechter, founder of the Gasthof Krone, – made his name as a lawyer in the Imperial service. In 1831 he was appointed as tutor to the sons of Archduke Charles. Later, the Emperor Francis Joseph I made him Director of the Coin and Antiques Cabinet in Vienna. He was ennobled by the Emperor to mark his completion of 40 years of service. During his scholarly career, Bergmann retained close emotional ties to the Hittisau community in which he had grown up. Reporting one of his last visits here, this time accompanied by the great Mozart scholar, Ritter von Köchel, Bergmann wrote on 13 August 1865 to his wife in Vienna:

"On Tuesday evening, the 8th, we reached Hittisau and took lodgings in the extremely comfortable Gasthaus zur Krone, proprietor Mr. Bechter, and found – as we still do – the food, rooms and beds to be of the best quality ... He [i.e. Köchel] likes it very much here; he accompanied me to visit my brothers, comes on the short walks with me daily, is thoroughly content with the pretty scenery and the charm of the countryside, with Mr. Bechter's house [i.e. the Krone], in a nutshell, with the country and the people in general, and feels so much at ease in this peaceful valley and lovely weather, that neither of us is in the least disposed to move elsewhere for the time being."

Früher war gestern …

1930 kaufen die Brüder Oskar und Walter Natter, in deren Besitz sich bereits die Post in Bezau befindet, die Hittisauer Krone. Bald darauf teilen sich die Brüder die Häuser auf, und Walter (1899 – 1971) übernimmt die Krone. Aus der Küche der Post holt er sich eine versierte Köchin …

Es kommt, wie es kommen muss, und man feiert Hochzeit. Appolonia, genannt Plone (1907 – 1980) reiht sich ein in die Liste der prominenten Kronenwirtinnen. Auf Wunsch ihres Gatten trug sie übrigens jahrein-jahraus die Bregenzerwälder Tracht, selbst im Sommer bei der schweißtreibenden Arbeit am großen Holzherd. 1934 kommt Tochter Erika zur Welt. Bald ist sie als rechte Hand ihrer Mutter überall in der Krone anzutreffen. Noch bevor ihr drei Jahre jüngerer Bruder Herbert das Haus übernimmt, amtiert sie einige Zeit lang als Kronenwirtin.

Langsam kommt das Geschäft nach dem Krieg wieder in Fahrt. An den Sonntagen füllen sich die Stuben zum Frühschoppen. Man trinkt Limonade, Flaschenbier (Fässer liefert die Brauerei nur an hohen Festtagen), Wein: Kalterer, Lagrein Kretzer, Gumpoldskirchner. Kriegsflüchtlinge aus dem Osten logieren im dritten Stock, ab und zu gibt es eine Hochzeit, einen Leichenschmaus. 1947/48 erste Bälle: die besseren Herrschaften fahren im Schlitten vor, Stallknechte spannen aus, versorgen die Rosse, im großen Kronensaal über dem Stall (heute Neubautrakt) wird getanzt, in den Stuben geschmaust: Schnitzel, Schweinsbraten, Hackbraten, Bratwürste mit Sauerkraut. Die Versorgung mit regionalen Produkten war damals mehr als ein Marketing-Schlagwort: es war eine notwendige Selbstverständlichkeit.

Mitte der 1950er Jahre werden das Herren- und das Südtirolerzimmer zum Speisesaal umgebaut. 1952 entsteht aus dem Geräteschuppen im hinteren Teil der Krone der Saal: Hier finden die berühmten Mittwoch-Tanzabende statt – über Jahre hinweg die wichtigste Partnerbörse des Vorderen Bregenzerwaldes. 1972 baut Herbert, der nach seiner Heirat mit Wilma vom Schwarzacher Engel zum Kronenwirt avanciert, die Kronen-Bar dazu und lockt damit Tanzwütige, Vergnügungssüchtige und Trinkfeste an.

*Bosnische Torte
nach Oma Plones Rezept*

8 Eier
250 g Staubzucker
250 g Haselnüsse gerieben
80 g Kochschokolade gewürfelt
40 g Zitronat oder Orangeat gewürfelt
1 Prise Salz

Eier in Eiweiss und Dotter trennen. Eiweiss mit dem Salz halbfest schlagen. Die Hälfte des Zuckers zugeben und cremig schlagen. Dann die übrigen Zutaten locker daruntermischen. In eine gefettete und bemehlte Form füllen und bei mässiger Hitze ca. 45 min. backen.

Once upon a time was only yesterday …

In 1930, brothers Oskar and Walter Natter – already owners of the Post at Bezau, purchased the Gasthof Krone at Hittisau. They soon split up their rights in the two establishments, with Walter (1899 – 1971) taking on the Krone. He also took on an experienced cook from the Post. Her name was Appolonia …

Things took their natural course, and the wedding bells rang out. Appolonia (1907 – 1980), usually Plone for short, joined the line of notable Krone landladies. To please her husband she wore the Bregenzerwald's traditional regional costume year in, year out, even for summertime work in the sweaty heat generated by the big wood-burning range. Plone's daughter Erika, born in 1934, quickly became her right-hand woman, here, there and everywhere in the Krone. When her brother Herbert, three years younger, took over, she had already been running the Krone for some time.

Once the war was over, trade gradually began to return. Sundays saw the Krone's public rooms crowded with pre-lunch social drinkers. On offer were lemonade, bottled beer (the breweries supplied draught beer only on high feast days), wines – Austrian Kalterer, Lagrein Kretzer, Gumpolds-kirchner. War refugees from the East were given shelter on the third floor. There were occasional weddings, and wakes. The first balls were held in 1947/48: the gentry drew up in sleighs, there were grooms to unhitch the horses and see to their hay and water; the dancing was in the Krone ballroom above the stable tract – where the new building is now; the Stuben or taprooms saw the feasting, with schnitzels, roast pork, meat loaf, bratwurst and sauerkraut. Regional sourcing of products used was no mere marketing buzzword in those days: with no other option, it was a fact of life.

The mid-1950s brought the conversion of the smoking-room and the South Tyrol-room into a dining room. In 1952 the tool-shed to the rear of the premises became a ballroom. This was the scene of the famous Wednesday night dances, which for years on end were the Lower Bregenzerwald's most

Bosnia Cake
Granny Plone's recipe

8 eggs
250 g icing sugar
250 g finely ground hazelnuts
80 g cooking chocolate, diced
40 g candied peel, lemon or orange
pinch salt

Separate the eggs.
Beat egg-whites and salt to form soft peaks. Add half the sugar and beat until creamy. Then lightly blend in the remaining ingredients. Pour the mix into a greased and floured form and bake in a moderate oven for about 45 minutes.

*Burgunderbraten –
ein richtiger
Kronen-Sonntagsbraten!*

1 Rindsschulter ca. 1 kg
Salz, Pfeffer, Senf
1 Zwiebel
2 Karotten
2 Knoblauchzehen
¼ Sellerieknollen
1 Scheibe Speck
2 Lorbeerblätter
1 EL Tomatenmark
½ l Rotwein
1 l Rindsuppe oder Kalbsjus
10 Pfefferkörner
5 Wacholderbeeren
1 Kräuterstrauss: ½ Lauchstange,
Petersilstengel, 2 Zweige Thymian
(Für 4 Personen)

*Die Rindsschulter mit Salz, Pfeffer und
Senf beidseitig würzen. Das Wurzelwerk
und den Speck würfelig schneiden.
Das Fleisch in Fett und einem EL
Butter beidseitig scharf anbraten, dann
herausheben.
Wurzelwerk mit dem Tomatenmark
kräftig anrösten. Mit Rotwein ablöschen
und etwas einkochen lassen. Suppe oder
Jus dazugiessen. Kräuter und Gewürze
zugeben und das Fleisch wieder einlegen.
Bei schwacher Hitze ca. 2 Stunden
dünsten. Mit Spätzle und Blaukraut oder
Fenchel servieren!*

In den frühen 1960er Jahren schwappt das deutsche Wirtschaftswunder in den Bregenzerwald über: Touristen kommen busweise aus dem Rheinland. Der günstige Wechselkurs des Franken bringt Schweizer Gäste ins Land. Für das Personal bedeutet das in erster Linie nicht enden wollende Arbeit: Berge von Geschirr und Tische voller Gläser, Körbe voller Wäsche: alles in Handarbeit mit dem auf dem großen Holzherd erhitzten Wasser zu spülen und zu waschen!

1966 wird die Stiege in den ersten Stock abgebrochen. Der Eingang in die Krone erfolgt nun vom Erdgeschoß aus, wo die Zollämter den bis heute existierenden Geschäften weichen. 1977 wird der nordseitige Saal abgerissen und unter der Federführung von Leopold Kaufmann durch Architekt Fritz Natter (* 1946), dem jüngsten Spross von Walter und Appolonia, umgebaut. Mit nunmehr 30 komfortablen Zimmern geht die Krone in eine neue Runde.

Hilda Eberle (*1929), die von 1946 – 1951 als Dienstmädchen in der Krone gearbeitet hat, erzählt aus dem Kronen-Alltag von dazumal: An Arbeit mangelte es nicht: Aufstehen um 6.00 Uhr, Sperrstunde und damit Feierabend um oder eben auch nach 22.00 Uhr, bei Bällen oder Hochzeiten in den Morgenstunden. Sieben Tage in der Woche. Urlaub: ein Fremdwort. Einziger Luxus: die tägliche Kaffeepause nachmittags um vier. Den Zucker in den Kaffee besorgt sich Hilda heimlich, d.h. sie versucht es ein Mal: Die Wirtin kriegt irgendwie Wind von der Sache und vertauscht wortlos die Tassen …

Und sogar nach fast durchgearbeiteter Samstagnacht ist der sonntägliche Kirchgang Dienstpflicht … Im Sommer produziert man im Keller Speiseeis. Zwei Sorten gibt es: Schoko und Vanille. Für jede bestellte Portion muss Hilda in den Keller hinuntersteigen. „Wenn nur das Wetter wieder einmal schlecht wäre", seufzt sie.

Mit dem neuen Jahrtausend steht der nächste Generationenwechsel in der Krone an. Helene, die jüngere Tochter von Herbert und Wilma, und ihr Mann Dietmar Nussbaumer übernehmen 2005 den Betrieb. Der im Herbst 2007 durchgeführte Umbau der Altbauzimmer in die Werkraumzimmer und die musterhaften modernen Wälderstuben läutet wiederum eine neue Kronen-Ära ein.

effective matchmaking facility. Herbert had married Wilma (of the Engel at Schwarzach) and subsequently become landlord of the Krone; in 1972 he had the Kronen-Bar added as an annex, so that there was encouragement for dance fanatics, revellers and carousers.

By the early 1960s, the German economic miracle was overflowing into the Bregenzerwald: busloads of tourists poured in from the Rhineland. The favourable exchange rate for the franc brought Swiss visitors too. For the staff of course it meant work, work, work: mountains of crockery, tables stacked with glasses, hamper upon hamper of laundry, and every last item had to be washed and rinsed by hand, in water heated on the great wood-fired range.

The steps up to the first storey were done away with in 1966. Now the Gasthof Krone entrance was at ground-floor level, where the excise offices gave way to the present shops. The north side hall was demolished in 1977 and rebuilt under the aegis of Leopold Kaufmann by the architect Fritz Natter (b. 1946), youngest scion of Walter and Appolonia. Now boasting 30 comfortable guest bedrooms, the Krone had entered on a new era.

Hilda Eberle (b. 1929) was a maid in the Krone from 1946 to 1951 and describes the daily routine in the Krone at the time. There was work aplenty – out of bed at 6 sharp, doors locked and hence the end of your day at 10 pm, or maybe later: if there was a dance or a wedding it would be the small hours. You worked seven days a week. Holidays – what's that? And just one single luxury: the coffee break every day at four. Hilda could sneak a drop of sugar into her coffee, or rather she tried it once; somehow the Krone's landlady got wind of the matter and, without saying a word, switched the cups …

You might work almost right through a Saturday night – but you still had to go to church on the Sunday … In summer they'd make icecream down in the basement. Two flavours – chocolate or vanilla. Every time someone ordered icecream, Hilda had to go down to the basement and fetch it. "How I longed for a bit of bad weather!" she sighs.

As the new millennium opened, the Krone's next changeover of generations was nearly due. Helene – younger daughter of Herbert and Wilma – and her husband Dietmar took over the business in 2005. The conversion of rooms in the old part of the building into the werkraum-designed new rooms and the superb modern Wälderstuben or Forest Rooms has ushered in yet another new era at the Gasthof Krone.

Burgundy Roast – this is a proper Krone Sunday roast!

approx. 1 kg shoulder of beef
salt, pepper, mustard
1 onion
2 carrots
2 cloves garlic
¼ celeriac
1 thick slice fat bacon
2 bay leaves
1 tbsp tomato puree
½ litre red wine
1 litre beef consomme or veal stock
10 peppercorns
5 juniper berries
1 bouquet garni: half a leek, parsley stalks, two sprigs thyme
(Serves 4)

Season the beef on both sides with the salt, pepper and mustard. Dice the root vegetables and the bacon. Brown the meat quickly on both sides in lard and 1 tbsp butter, then remove from pan. Sear the root vegetables with the tomato puree added. Pour on the red wine and allow to simmer a while. Add the consomme or stock. Add the herbs and spices, then put the meat back in. Braise on a low setting for about 2 hours. Serve with spaetzle noodles and either red cabbage or fennel.

Die Krone in den 1920er Jahren, weitgehend der Originalzustand des Hauses: mit den Zollämtern im Erdgeschoß, dem zweiseitigen Stiegenaufgang in den ersten Stock, dem Stall im rückwärtigen Teil. Von seiner Wirkung hat der mächtige Bau in den 170 Jahren seines Bestehens nichts verloren.

The Krone in the 1920s, still retaining most of the original structure and layout, with the excise offices at street level, the converging flights of outside steps up to the first floor and the stables at the rear. The huge building has lost none of its grandeur over the 170 years of its life.

Gasthof und Hotel seit 1838. Die Krone in Hittisau – denn Kronengasthäuser gibt es allein schon in der näheren Umgebung einige und jede Krone pocht naturgemäß auf ihre Einzigartigkeit – die Krone in Hittisau, um die es in diesem Buch geht: Wer ist sie?

Die Krone in Hittisau

Ein 170 Jahre altes mächtiges Holzhaus direkt am Dorfplatz in nunmehr teilweise neuem Gewand. Seit kurzer Zeit in den Händen der dritten Generation: die Tochter Helene und ihr Gatte Dietmar mitsamt ihrer gut 15 köpfigen Kronenfamilie in Küche, Service, Büro oder Etage schaffen eine Atmosphäre, die mit Freundlichkeit, Professionalität, Gastfreundschaft, usw. nur halb beschrieben wird. Die andere Hälfte besteht aus der Selbstverständlichkeit, mit der man hier den Gästen begegnet: keine aufgesetzte Höflichkeit, sondern ein Selbstbewusstsein, das die Gäste trägt und von ihnen getragen wird.

In diesem Geist gedeiht alles weitere, was die Krone ist:

Eine seit Jahrzehnten von den Einheimischen und aus nah und fern angereisten Gästen geschätzte Küche, dekoriert von maßgeblichen Gourmet- und Restaurantführern. Zu genießen Tag für Tag im Restaurant oder im Rahmen von Gourmet-Wochenenden, Themenabenden mit großen Menüs, speziellen Oster- oder Weihnachtsarrangements. Ein unprätentiöser, aber anspruchsvoller Weinkeller mit einer ausgewogenen Auswahl österreichischer Winzer. Ehrliche Qualität mit dem Ziel, den Gästen mit einem attraktiven Preis-Leistungsverhältnis zu begegnen.

The Krone has been a Gasthof (inn) and hotel since 1838. The Krone at Hittisau – one needs to remember there are several Krone hostelries nearby, and each one of course insists on its particular uniqueness – the Krone at Hittisau, which this book is about: who and what is it?

The Krone at Hittisau

It is a massive, 170-year-old wood-built house right on the village square, with parts now newly clad. For not very long now it has been in the hands of the third-generation owners – the daughter, Helene, and her husband Dietmar with their Gasthof Krone family, fully 15 strong, in the kitchen, in bar or restaurant, office or room service – all combining to create an ambiance that is only half described by calling it friendly, professional, welcoming, and so on. The other half is the matter-of-fact way in which staff relate to guests: no false deference here, but a confident bearing expressive of mutual respect between staff and guests.

It is in this spirit that all else thrives naturally at the Krone, in particular:

Superb cuisine that has been prized for decades past by local people and by visitors from near and far, holder of awards from leading gastronomy and restaurant guides. It is there to be enjoyed every day in the restaurant, or alternatively in the context of gourmet weekends, themed evenings with extended menus, or special packages offered at Christmas and Easter. An unpretentious, yet classy wine cellar featuring a well-balanced range of Austrian growers. Honest-to-goodness quality based on our policy of offering guests attractive value for money.

Der typische Kronengast liebt Crème brûlée ebenso wie Kalbsbeuschel, hausgemachten Topfenstrudel oder Sibratsgfäller Forellen im Ganzen gebraten, geschmorte Lammhaxe oder Subirerparfait, ein Ziegenkäsle mit Walnusskruste und Rosmarin-Honigsirup oder ein Filet vom Almochsen, ein lauwarmes Kalbszüngle mit Ruccola und Senfvinaigrette oder ein Bodensee-Zanderfilet, eine Linsencrèmesuppe mit Hirschschinken oder Selleriesalat mit geräucherter Entenbrust. Dazu etwa einen Grünen Veltliner aus der Wachau oder einen Blaufränkischen aus dem Burgenland.

Die Kronengäste lieben die gute alte Kronenstube und nicht wenige erleben derzeit eine stürmisch-romantische Affaire mit den umgebauten Räumen. Die ca. 90 Sitzplätze reichen meistens, aber nicht immer. Im Sommer ist die Terrasse mit Blick über den Dorfplatz ein gesuchter Treffpunkt für Feinschmeckerinnen oder Müßiggänger und nicht nur an lauschigen Abenden sind die 24 Plätze (fast) so begehrt wie die Blaue (oder die Rote?) Mauritius …

Ess-, Trink-, Tischkultur: wie überhaupt Kultur werden groß geschrieben in der Krone. Hochkarätige CDs und HiFi-Anlagen in den neuen Zimmern und eine kleine Bibliothek möchten kreative Muße und produktive Einkehr fördern. Literarische Abende geben weit mehr ab als bloßen Hintergrund für die Höhenflüge der Küche. Bald startet eine hochkarätig besetzte Gesprächsreihe mit gesellschafts- und kulturpolitisch relevanten Themen. Die Krone pflegt enge Kooperationen mit der Schubertiade Schwarzenberg und mit dem Hittisauer Frauenmuseum.

Die Krone ist Mitglied der MundArt-Betriebe: Acht Gasthöfe/Hotels im Bregenzerwald mit einer gemeinsamen Überzeugung: Qualität, Authentizität, Tradition, Herzlichkeit, Natur, Komfort, Romantik, Genuss, Regionalität als verbindende Elemente.

Exklusiv für Hausgäste gibt es eine kleine Sauna; einen schattigen Garten zum Entspannen, Lesen, Plaudern, für stille Mußestunden oder ein kleines Tischtennismatch zwischendurch; ein Kaminzimmer mit Bibliothek: sommers und winters ein beliebter Ort für einen geselligen Apéro, eine wärmende Teestunde, einen kühlen Drink, eine spannende Partie Schach oder ein kniffliges Kartenspiel, ein ausführliches Gespräch oder eine fröhliche Runde …

Und weil das Leben nicht nur aus Urlaub besteht: warten in der Krone helle und moderne Seminar- und Tagungsräume mit kompletter technisch-medialer Ausstattung und umfassender persönlicher und kulinarischer Betreuung für bis zu 25 Personen.

„Wenn ich der Abwesenheitsstatistik meiner Frau glaube, bin ich im Jahr mindestens 150 Tage unterwegs. Unsere Unternehmensgruppe arbeitet in 40 Ländern und ich übernachte in den verschiedensten Hotels weltweit. Es gibt aber nur ganz wenige Hotels, die wirklich etwas Besonderes sind, die es schaffen, dass sich der Gast sofort wohl fühlt wie zuhause. Die Krone in Hittisau ist so ein Hotel mit einem besonderen Geist, geprägt von der Herzlichkeit der Menschen, die dort arbeiten, der ausgezeichneten Küche und der wunderbaren Umgebung. Die Krone ist etwas Besonderes und ich bin sehr froh, dass ich dort manchmal Gast sein darf … und das auch mit meiner Frau, denn gemeinsame Abwesenheit zählt nicht für die Statistik."
Reiner Pichler, CEO Strellson AG

The typical guest at the Krone loves such things as Crème brûlée, veal offal, homemade quark strudel, local Sibratsgfäll trout grilled whole, braised lamb shank or pear schnaps parfait, a goat cheese round with walnut crust and rosemary-and-honey syrup or a fillet of alpine-grazed beef, a veal tongue served warm with rocket and a mustard-based vinaigrette, or a Lake Constance pike-perch fillet, or cream of lentil soup with cold cuts of venison, or celeriac salad with smoked breast of duck. And to accompany the meal, perhaps a Grüner Veltliner from the Wachau or a Blaufränkisch red from Burgenland.

The Krone's regulars and new guests love the good old Krone Stube to eat and drink in, and quite a few have fallen passionately for the newly rebuilt accommodation. There is seating for about 90 – usually this is enough, but not always. The terrace area overlooking the village square is a favourite summertime rendezvous for gourmets and for those with time on their hands, and it is not only on mild cosy evenings that the 24 seats are as sought-after (well, nearly!) as Centre Court seats for Wimbledon finals.

The culture of gastronomy, of fine wines, of dining as a social art... Culture in its best forms is a strong point at the Krone. High-quality CDs and hi fi in the new rooms and a small library are there to help ensure your leisure is creative, your "quiet times" productive. Literary evenings here are far more than mere alibis for riding high on the cuisine. We will soon be launching a social and cultural discussion forum with big-name panellists. The Krone already liaises actively with both the Schubertiade (Schubert Festival) at Schwarzenberg and the Women's Museum here in Hittisau.

The Krone belongs to the MundArt business grouping of eight Bregenzerwald Gasthöfe or hotels linked by their core values: quality, authenticity, tradition, welcome, nature, comfort, romantic appeal, enjoyment of good things, regional identification.We have a small sauna reserved exclusively for our house guests; a garden with shade to relax in, or read, or chat, or just enjoy the peace or a spot of table-tennis; and a room with a library of books where you can sit by the fireside in winter. Summer or winter, this is a popular place to enjoy an aperitif with friends, a cheering afternoon tea, a long cool drink, a tense chess match or a tricksy game of cards ... or settle down for a long talk ... or celebrate meeting up again with your friends ...And as life can't be all holidays, the Krone has bright, modern seminar and conference accommodation ready and waiting, equipped with full multimedial faciities. Comprehensive personal and catering services are available for up to 25 people.

"If I am to believe my wife's record of my time away, the total is at least 150 days in the year. Our Group operates in 40 different countries, and I find myself staying in an extraordinarily wide range of hotels worldwide. Very few indeed of them are truly something special, a hotel in which somehow the guest can arrive and feel at ease right away just as one does at home. The Krone at Hittisau is just that sort of hotel. There is a special feel about it, from the warmth and friendliness of the staff, and then the excellent food and the lovely countryside around. The Krone is something special, and I am very happy that I get to stay there sometimes ... which includes coming with my wife, because when she comes too it doesn't count in her log of my days away."
Reiner Pichler, CEO of Strellson AG

Die Krone in Hittisau ist eine gewachsene Anlage. In den 170 Jahren ihres Bestehens hat sie sich schon einige Male gewandelt. Das bisher letzte Mal beim massiven Umbau in den 1970er Jahren, der nicht nur im nördlichen Teil deutliche Spuren hinterließ. Auch an der Südseite des Hauses waren es gerade die Elemente dieser Zeit, die mittlerweile in die Jahre gekommen sind, abgenutzt wirkten oder funktionell nicht mehr entsprachen.

Miteinander von Alt und Neu

Architekt Bernardo Bader

Übergeordnetes Ziel der Arbeit war es, mit jedem Eingriff den baulichen Altbestand wieder mehr zum Strahlen zu bringen. Uns war klar, dass für eine solche Bauaufgabe viel Sensibilität erforderlich ist; aber auch die Absicht und der Mut, Neues im Haus zu wagen, beseelten uns. Eine besondere Art des Miteinanders von Alt und Neu schwebte uns von Anfang an vor, die nicht geprägt sein sollte von starken Kontrasten und dramatischen Konfrontationen, vielmehr von der Freude am Gewachsenen und Heterogenen. Es sollten baukünstlerische Synergien entstehen, die eben nur der spezielle Kontext zulässt.

Äusseres Erscheinungsbild/Eingang
Wie unterschiedlich dosiert dieses Miteinander ausfallen kann, verdeutlicht die äußere Gestaltungsaufgabe. Waren es an der Frontfassade der Rückbau der ehemaligen Saalfenster, das Anbringen neuer frischer Lamellenläden oder ein revitalisiertes Wirtshausschild, so war bei der Eingangssituation deutlich mehr Gestaltungsaufwand erforderlich.

Der ehemalige stirnseitige zweiläufige Aufgang vom Dorfplatz in den Mittelflur – typisch für das ursprüngliche Haus des Vorderen Bregenzerwaldes – war bereits in den 60er Jahren einer grossen Terrasse gewichen. Die behäbig wirkenden dunklen Einbauten im vormaligen Kellergeschoss wurden durch eine helle hölzerne Figur ersetzt. In möbelartiger Perfektion gearbeitet, erklärt diese nunmehr den Eingang und transportiert den Gast nach oben.

Bauherrschaft/Architekt/Handwerker/Projektbeteiligte
Es ist meiner Meinung nach ein Fehler, die Architektur oder die Ästhetik bei einem Bauherren- oder Handwerkergespräch in den Vordergrund zu stellen. Vielmehr ist es nötig – und als Ausgangspunkt der Arbeit als Architekt auch spannender – mit den Menschen über ihre ureigensten Kompetenzen zu sprechen: mit den Bauherren über das Funktionieren des Hauses, ihre Wünsche und nicht zuletzt über ökonomische Grenzen; mit den Handwerkern über funktionierende, erprobte Ausführungen oder traditionelle Handwerksmethoden.

The Krone at Hittisau has grown organically. In the 170 years of its life so far it has already undergone several transformations. The last of these was the major reconstruction undertaken in the 1970s, which left its mark on the north side of the premises, though not only there. On the south front of the building it was the work done at this time that had begun to age noticeably, with some parts looking run-down and shabby, or no longer fulfilling a useful purpose.

Old and New in harmony

Bernardo Bader, architect

Our over-riding priority was that every change we made should help bring out the former beauty of the building's historic structure. Obviously this meant any structural work would need to be handled with great sensitivity. And yet we were also determined to risk doing something new in the building, and had the confidence to go ahead. Right from the start we envisaged a special way of juxtaposing old and new, avoiding full-on contrasts and dramatic confrontations and concentrating rather on the appeal of a building that has developed organically and heterogeneously over time. The idea was to bring out architectural synergies that could come about only in this particular context.

External appearance/Entrance
This heterogeneity can turn out to have widely differing consequences, as was illustrated by the external design issues. Where the front façade only involved dismantling the windows of the old hall, fitting bright new Venetian shutters or a refurbished inn sign, the entrance area clearly needed more design input.

The two flights of steps that once led up at the front from the village square to the central hallway – characteristic of the Lower Bregenzerwald vernacular style – had been replaced in the 1960s by a large terrace area. The dark-toned and rather bulky structures at the old basement level were replaced by a light-coloured wooden surround. This feature, which is finished to a furniture-like standard of perfection, now lightens the entrance and ushers the arriving guest upwards.

Clients/Architect/Craftworkers/Project participants
I believe it is a mistake to focus too much on the architecture or aesthetics of a project when talking to either the clients or the craftsmen. What matters – and this also makes for a more stimulating starting-point for the architect's work – is to talk to people about where their real, quintessential competences lie: with the clients you discuss how the building is to function, what their wishes are, and, not least, the budget; and you talk to the working craftsmen and women about tried functional solutions or about traditional craft methods.

Eine in möbelartiger Perfektion gearbeitete hölzerne Figur erklärt den Eingang und transportiert den Gast förmlich nach oben. Teppich und Decke verlaufen von Aussen nach Innen und sind unmerklich durch die Glastüre getrennt. Neuer Stubenflügel im ersten Obergeschoss mit stubenartiger, halboffener Grundrisskonfiguration bietet Platz für den Gast des Hauses, aber auch für den heimischen Wirthausgänger.

A wooden surround, much like a perfectly finished piece of furniture, declares the entrance and literally whisks the guest upstairs. Carpet and ceiling provide the transition from the outside to the inside, imperceptibly separated by a glass door. The new Stuben wing on the first floor in stuben-like, half-open groundplan configuration welcomes hotel residents and local regulars alike.

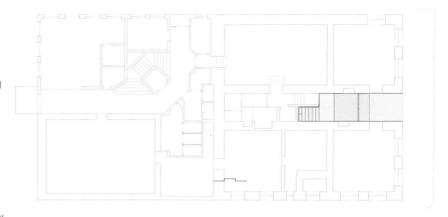

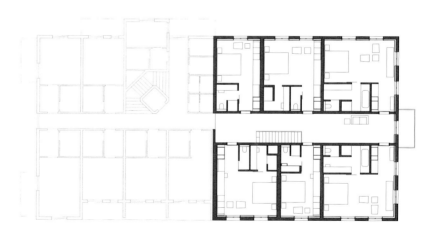

Im Kopfteil des Hauses schließt nach oben eine wohnzimmerartige Gangzone die vertikale Erschliessung ab. Basierend auf der statischen Grundkonfiguration des traditionellen Holz – Strickbaus formen sich 6 neue Zimmer.

At the gable end of the house, the vertical development concludes with a livingroom-like hall area. Six new rooms take shape, based on the static basic configuration of the traditional blockhouse construction.

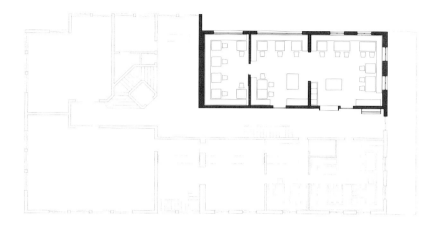

Die alten südwestseitig im ersten Obergeschoss gelegenen Stuben sind die gut funktionierende und stark nachgefragte Basis des Hauses. Der links des traditionellen Mittelflurs liegende offene Saal hatte mit funktionellen und mit atmosphärischen Problemen zu kämpfen. Durch einen teilweisen Rückbau in den Belangen Raumstruktur, Fassadenbild und Oberflächenqualitäten entstanden neue stubenartige, halboffene Situationen. Ziel war es, die geforderten Funktionen des hausinternen Frühstücksbuffets und des à-la-carte-Betriebes aufnehmen zu können. Es erschien uns aber auch wichtig, hier in zentraler Lage Raum für Hochzeiten, Versammlungen und Familienfeste zu schaffen. Die einzelnen Gaststuben wurden dem historischen Bestand folgend mit einfachen gebürsteten Fichten- oder Weisstannen-Massivholzvertäfelungen (Fries und Füllung) ausgestattet. Wir waren bestrebt, mit traditionellen handwerklichen Methoden eine zeitgemäße Aussage zu treffen.

The old Stuben (public rooms) located in the southwestern part of the first floor are the heart of the hotel, very heavily used and still wholly fit for purpose. The large open hall to the left of the traditional central hallway was problematic in terms of practical usability, and there were ventilation issues. Partial dismantling affecting the room structure, the façade appearance and the finishing produced new, roomy, semi-open spaces. The objective was to create suitable settings for the residents' breakfast buffet and the à-la-carte restaurant. However, we also felt it was important to create sufficient space here for wedding receptions, large meetings and family celebrations. In keeping with the historic furnishings of the house, the various public rooms were finished in simple brushed spruce or silver fir solid panelling (frieze and infill). We were aiming to produce a thoroughly contemporary statement, but by using traditional craft methods.

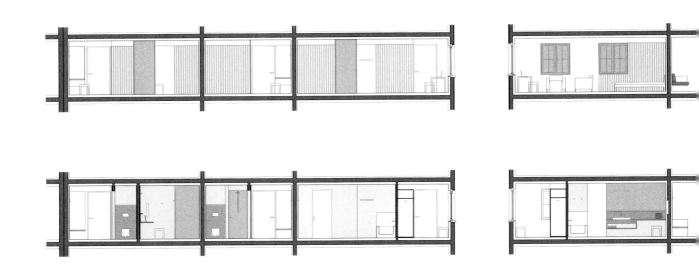

Ein neuer wohnzimmerartig gestalteter Flur erschliesst die sechs neu gestalteten Zimmer. Die Intimität nimmt, aus den Gaststuben kommend und über den Wohnzimmergang in das Zimmer eintretend, zu. Ähnlich einem Schneckenhaus endet die Raumspirale im intimsten Raum – eben im Badezimmer; hier wird man, am dialektischen Höhepunkt des Spieles von Alt und Neu, nach dem Wandel durch das Haus gewissermaßen geerdet. Die Zimmerzonen mit den handwerklich perfekt gearbeiteten Massivholzmöbeln und den intarsienartigen Wandvertäfelungen sind zwar neu interpretiert, aber stark mit dem Geist des Hauses verwachsen.

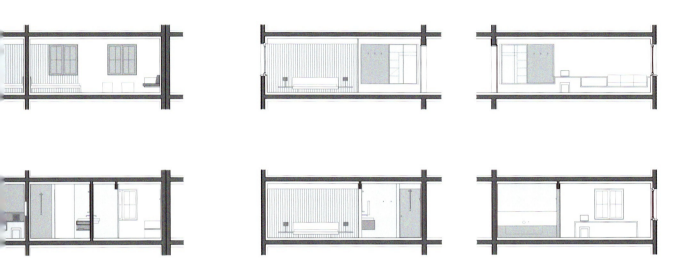

A new landing styled like a sitting room leads to the six new-design guest bedrooms. The sense of intimacy grows as one leaves the public rooms and makes one's way across the sittingroom-like landing to one's bedroom. As in a snail-shell, the spiral of rooms ends in the most private room, here the bathroom; and here too at last, at the climax of the dialectic between the old and the new, and after, passing through the building, one has, so to speak, finally gone to ground. The bedroom zones with their perfectly crafted solid wood furniture and intarsia-style wall panelling, though newly interpreted, are strongly redolent of the building's continuing spirit.

Florian Aicher

Krone-Umbau

Krone Alterations

Unsichtbare Kräfte

Betritt man den Raum – besser wäre vielleicht: einen solchen Zustand – so kann man eigentlich nur die Hände über dem Kopf zusammenschlagen und Reißaus nehmen: Einer einzigen Wunde gleicht, was seit einigen Tagen Baustelle ist. Aufgerissene Wände entblößen den Bau, abgebrochene Decken und herausgerissene Böden legen das Gerippe des Hauses frei, Kabel und Leitungen lösen sich, gekappten Blut- und Nervensträngen gleich, aus dem Gewebe der Wände, prothesenartig ist all das von einem Gerüst umfangen. Wie kann da ein Mensch nur durchblicken! Doch als wäre der Zustand nicht genug: Das Bild bewegt sich, zwei bis drei Dutzend Menschen sind mit etwas beschäftigt, werken ohne Unterlass, konzentriert und doch fast traumwandlerisch, flink und doch nie aufgeregt, kraftvoll und doch kaum laut – merkwürdig der Sound eines solchen Raumes: An- und Auslaufen von akkugetriebenen Elektromotoren, Sägen, Bohren, gelegentlich Hämmern, das Piepsen von Lasermessgeräten in wechselnder Tonhöhe, kaum ein Zuruf. Wie von Geisterhand gelenkt geht ein jeder seinem Geschäft nach, als wisse er von Haus aus, was zu tun ist, als bedürfe es keiner Worte. Doch genau besehen ordnet sich das Bild, und aus diesem wie am Schnürchen laufenden Getriebe lösen sich Gruppen und ausgeprägte Gestalten.

Da sind die, deren Werken und Wirken später vom Bau verschluckt zu sein scheint, etwa: die Abbrucharbeiter, die den Bestand zerlegen und sortieren. Oder die Elektriker („Bin der Erste und der Letzte auf der Baustelle"), die das Geschehen Tag für Tag wie ein leiser Ton begleiten, vorauseilend mit dem Abklemmen, dann jedem auf den Fersen mit dem Verlegen von Leerrohren (hier rund 2 km) und Einziehen der Leitungen, gefolgt vom Anschluss aller Arten von Steuerung, Schaltung, Sicherung, um mit der Montage der letzten Lampen die Baustelle zu übergeben. Oder: der Installateur, dem der Gast verdankt, dass der Raum behaglich temperiert ist, dass auf Handbewegung Wasser aus der Leitung sprudelt, Maß und Temperatur nach Wunsch – all das im Verborgenen und wohlüberlegt zugeführt nach den Plänen des Meisters, der das Gedächtnis des Hauses genannt wird, weil er nicht nur all das im Kopf hat, sondern alle Leitungen und Muffen kennt, die in den letzten 150 Jahren hier verlegt wurden, und der mit seinem Wissen die Baustelle prägt. Da sind die Zimmerleute, deren Zugriff und Wille nicht nur die eigene Arbeit, sondern die ganze Baustelle vorantreibt, die in fliegendem Wechsel überall zupacken, tragende Wände „stricken" (Strickbau wird der Blockbau hier genannt wegen der verzahnten Fügung rechtwinkliger verbauter Hölzer, dies erst verleiht Stabilität), wertvolle Holzverkleidung sichern, Treppen erneuern, Wände „schiften" (Unterbau, in Lot und Wasser) und dämmen, Böden vergüten. Das wird abgeschlossen von den Betonbauern, die einem Überfallkommando gleich die Baustelle besetzen, jeden anderen hinausdrängen ohne nach

Der hier übliche Ausdruck **stricken** wird in Gebrauch gewesen sein lange bevor G. Semper vor 150 Jahren seine bahnbrechende Theorie, wonach Textilverarbeitung grundlegend für das Bauen sei, in dem Stichwort bündelte: „Aus der Naht eine Tugend machen".

Invisible forces

Walk on to the site one day – I'm tempted to say "Get yourself into a state like this" – and really all you can do is wring your hands and go somewhere else instead. What looks like an enormous physical wound is just the building site a few days after the start. Walls have been torn open showing the construction, broken ceilings and ripped-out floors expose the building's structural frame, cables and piping dangle from the wall fabric like severed blood-vessels and tendons, and the whole thing wears its scaffolding like a giant calliper. How is anyone to make sense of it all? And as if this image of chaos were not enough in itself, it is actually a moving image, two or three dozen people are working on something, busy busy, intensely focused on what they are doing and yet almost as if sleep-walking, moving nimbly but never excitedly, vigorously but hardly that you would hear them – odd, the sound pattern you do get from a place like that – hand-held electric tools whining and cutting off, sawing, drills, sometimes hammering, bleeping at different pitches – that's from the laser measuring tools – and hardly ever a human voice raised. It's as if they were all controlled by magic, every one of them going about his business as if he'd always known what needed doing, no need for words. But then you really look properly, and the picture resolves itself, and this smoothly whirring machine turns out to be made up of groups and distinctive individual figures.

There are some there whose effort and activity seem later on to have been swallowed up and vanished – like the demolition team taking the fabric apart and sorting the materials. Or the electricians ("I'm first in and I'm last off the site"), who are in on the action day after day like a faint background hum, rushing to pinch off and then following hard on everyone's heels putting in the conduits (over a mile of them) and threading the cables in, then after that installing every possible control device, switchgear, fuseboxes, all so that the minute the last reading-lamp goes in the whole site can be handed over. Or: the plumber – he's the one the hotel guest can thank for a room that is just at a nice temperature to sit in, that a touch of the hand brings water gushing out of the tap, how much and how hot just as desired – all that goes in unseen but meticulously following the plan of the master plumber, who's called the house memory because not only has he got all this in his head, but he also knows about every pipe and conduit, every coupler installed here in the last 150 years, and it's his knowledge that makes the building site tick. Then there are the carpenters ... Their work and their motivation drives the whole site forward, you see them piling in everywhere, one goes off, colleague in right away; they are "knitting" the load-bearing walls (it's blockhouse construction, but they call it "knitting" here because of the way timbers meeting at right angles are made to mesh together, that's what gives the stability); putting good wood panelling to one side, rebuilding staircases, ensuring the walls are

The term **stricken**, widely used here, (literally "knitting") will have been current long before the time, 150 years back, when G. Semper summed up his groundbreaking theory that textile processes are basic to building too in his adaptation of the tag about "making a virtue of necessity [aus der Not]" to " ... of needlework [aus der Naht]".

links oder rechts zu sehen, in straffem Rhythmus den Betonbrei ausbreiten, nivellieren, abziehen (wobei immer wieder in Erstaunen versetzt, wie sicher Auge und Übung bemessen, was das Lasergerät nur noch bestätigt: Menge und Konsistenz), so dass am folgenden Tag die neue Ebene begehbar ist und heutige Ansprüche des Brandschutzes, der Statik, der Akustik mit einem Mal erledigt sind. Dann der Trockenbauer, der neue Wände und Decken einzieht, die Aufmerksamkeit in Person, ohne Unterlass lauernd auf eigene und fremde Fehler, vom Unterbau an, immer den Abschluss auch durch fremde Gewerke mitdenkend und auf unbedingte Verlässlichkeit bedacht (keine Wand, die nicht doppelt beplankt wäre).

Inmitten dieser klar zu unterscheidenden Gruppen und Figuren: der Bauleiter. Er vermittelt, gibt Auskunft, packt an, ist da. Allrounder, Springer, Kontroller, Bauführer und mehr, weil nicht auf eine Funktion beschränkt; die Zeichnung, den Terminplan im Kopf, immer ein offenes Ohr für den Bauherrn, die letzte Bemerkung des Architekten gegenwärtig. Doch kein Kommandieren, sondern Vorankommen möglich machen mit offenem Auge, Wissen um die Schritte der anderen, Bedingungen herstellen, damit sie schaffen können, mit der Bereitstellung von Material, Arbeit und Zeit beginnend und mit der Sicherstellung der Entsorgung noch längst nicht endend, dabeisein von frühmorgens bis Feierabend. Er bildet das Rückgrat der Baustelle, das zentrale Organ, das aus dem Vorbewussten lenkt und leitet.

Wenn es den Geist oder die Seele auszeichnet, dass man ihrer nicht habhaft wird, dass sie erscheint und wieder entschwindet, sich mit Fragen bemerkbar macht, wünscht, anregt, zu bedenken gibt, sich sorgt, immer da und doch nicht greifbar, überflüssig nach Lehrbuch und in einer geplanten Welt undenkbar und doch wirklich weil wirksam – hier gibt's das leibhaftig: Ansporn, Maßstab, Vorbild, Geistesgegenwart. Die Rede ist vom Wirt, vom Bauherrn, dessen Präsenz ihren Höhepunkt erreicht, wenn er und seine Frau alle Bauarbeiter täglich zur selben Zeit in die beste Gaststube zum Mittagstisch bitten. Immer frisch aufgekocht, mit Suppe vor dem Hauptgang und Kaffee danach, wobei der Hausherr es sich nicht nehmen lässt, zu bedienen. So stellt man Wertschätzung tätig dar, und nichts macht deutlicher als solcher Dank, bei wem dieses Unternehmen seinen Ausgang und sein Ende nimmt. Hier am Tisch wird täglich genährt, was die Seele des Ganzen ist, die in der Brust eines jeden Beteiligten schlägt – und mit den Worten des Polsterers etwa so klingt: „Engagierte Bauherrn gehören ja bei mir zum Geschäft, aber die Kronenleute, die sind mehr dabei, mit mehr Gefühl, kennen den Gast, prüfen, sind unwahrscheinlich dahinter, lassen sich nicht alles sagen, auch nicht vom Architekt. Da tue ich mich leichter, wenn jemand im Beruf mitten drin steht, in der Küche, sein Handwerk beherrscht wie wir – der ist feinfühliger."

(substructure, has to be plumb) and insulating them, making good the floors. And this is rounded off by the concrete team, they take over the site like a military operation, hustle everyone else off regardless, then in strict tempo spread out their cement mix, level it, screed it off (and it is always amazing how they know by eye and experience what the laser thing just confirms for them: the amount and the consistency) – so that the new-laid surface is usable next morning and conforms once and for all to present-day requirements for fire-resistance, structural strength, sound insulation. Then the timber erector, putting up new walls and ceilings, watchfulness personified, ever on the lookout for mistakes, his own or by others, all the way from the substructure upwards, always alert to the consequences even of work done by unrelated trades, and mindful of the need for total reliability (no wall without double panelling).

In the midst of all these well-defined teams and individuals, a single figure: the site engineer. He keeps different groups in touch, dispenses advice, lends a hand when needed, is always there. All-rounder, stand-in anywhere, controller, foreman and more, because he's multi-functional; he has the blueprints and completion schedule in his head, always time to listen to the client, architect's latest comment at his fingertips. But no ordering people around; instead he keeps things moving by having his eyes open, knowing what others are up to, creating the conditions for people to work, starting by ensuring that materials, work and time are available, still nothing like finished when he's got the day's site rubbish away; on site every day from first thing until work ends. He is the spinal column of the building site, the central organ with the necessary foreknowledge to guide and direct.

If it is the mark of the spirit or soul to be elusive, to appear and vanish again, to get itself noticed by asking questions, to wish, to suggest, to remind, to worry, always there and yet intangible, superfluous according to the textbooks, unthinkable in a planned world, yet real because producing effects – here we have all this in physical, bodily form: stimulus, yardstick, role-model, presence of mind. The description is of the landlord, the client, never more present than when he and his wife, every day at the same hour, invite all the site workers into the best Stube for their midday meal. Always freshly cooked, soup and main course, coffee to follow, which the master of the house insists on serving personally. This is how one actively shows one's respect, and nothing shows more clearly than this act of gratitude just where the great undertaking begins and ends. At this board, nourishment is provided for the heart and soul of the whole thing, alive and beating in all concerned – and expressed, in the words of the upholsterer, roughly like this: "I have plenty of clients who take a real interest, but the Krone people are more into things, more emotionally involved, they know their hotel guests, they check things out, they're incredibly clued up, don't take people's word for it, not even the architect's. It's easier for me if the person's a real professional, in the kitchen, knows his job inside out like we do – then he'll be more understanding."

werkraum

Der Name **werkraum** knüpft an eine Tradition von Initiativen an, die sich Qualität in Handwerk und Gestaltung verpflichtet haben: Die vereinigten Werkstätten und Werkbünde um 1900, die Werkstättenpädagogik des Bauhauses um 1920, alle wiederum W. Morris und J. Ruskin um 1860 folgend.

Dass dies hier nicht irgendein Umbau wird, haben die Wirtsleute schon lange gewusst – und sich rechtzeitig der Handwerker des „werkraum" vergewissert samt sorgfältigster Planung durch einen Architekten. Und auch hier: nicht Auftrag, um sich eigener Präsenz zu entledigen, sondern: immer dabei, unterstützt und beraten nur durch die Besten.

Ein solches Urteil darf sich der werkraum nach rund 10-jähriger Tätigkeit auf die Fahnen schreiben: auf dem Gebiet des Hausbaus, der Einrichtung, des Möbelbaus die Besten der Region in seinen Reihen zu vereinen. Handwerkliche Qualität, gestalterische Standfestigkeit und der Wille, sich von altem und neuem Plunder, den der Tourismus ins Land geweht hat, zu befreien, führte damals die (heute nicht mehr ganz jungen) jungen Wilden des Handwerks zusammen und regte zu außergewöhnlichen Aktionen an: eine eigene Zeitschrift, vier international besetzte und beachtete Gestaltungswettbewerbe, Initiativen zur Ausbildung und immer wieder Öffentlichkeitsarbeit. Dabei standen stets Schöpfungen der Mitglieder anschaulich und handgreiflich im Mittelpunkt und haben nun in Wien, München, Paris und weiter den besten Ruf. Was draußen mindestens ebenso Aufsehen erregt: dass es auf diese Weise gelungen ist, dem Handwerk in dieser Region zu öffentlichem Ansehen, Respekt und also kaum zu stillender Nachfrage zu verhelfen, was eine Blüte handwerklicher Kultur hervortrieb, von der man andernwärts bestenfalls träumt.

Das Zusammenspiel der Handwerksbetriebe und einer Bauherrenschaft, die sich ihren Kunstsinn nicht gänzlich durch den Geldinstinkt hat austreiben lassen, bringt die vielbestaunte Vitalität des Kulturraums Bregenzerwald hervor – ein Gemeinschaftswerk, das immer wieder von engagierten Einzelnen belebt wird. So auch im vorliegenden Fall, wo sich Wirtsleute sehr bewusst für die Handwerker des werkraum entschieden haben. „Natürlich gab es immer Beispiele, wo wir zusammengearbeitet haben" berichtet der örtliche Tischler, „aber hier, da ging es vom Kopf aus, von den Wirtsleuten. Die wollten ein richtiges werkraum-Menü."

The werkraum

The proprietors of the Krone have long been aware that this was not going to be any old make-do-and-mend makeover, and made sure in good time that they could secure craft workers from the werkraum, as well as meticulous professional planning by an architect. Here too commissioning the work was not a way of avoiding involvement. On the contrary, they were always around, supported and advised only by the best.

Roughly 10 years into its life, the werkraum can justly claim that it has brought together the region's best craftworkers in the areas of house-building, fitting and furnishing, and cabinet-making. High-level craftsmanship, consistency of design and the determination to break free from the tat washed into the area by the tourist flood were what brought together the Young Turks of the crafts industry (now rather less young) and spurred them into some exceptional initiatives: their own journal, four design competitions that drew international participation and attention; training initiatives, and constant attention to publicity. They saw to it that products created by the members were visibly and tangibly there at centre stage, and by now they enjoy the best of reputations in Vienna, Munich, Paris and further afield. What arouses at least as much interest out there is that they succeeded in this way in bringing the region's handcraft work to public notice and respect, and so also to a near insatiable demand for it; this in turn produced a flowering of the culture of craftsmanship such as other regions could only dream about.

The productive relationship between the handcraft businesses and their client base – among which artistic taste has not been wholly displaced by the profit motive – is the crucial factor that has brought the much admired vitality of the Bregenzerwald region's culture to its present prominence. It is a communal enterprise infused again and again with fresh vigour by committed individuals. The Krone rebuild is a case in point, the owners having made a considered decision to engage werkraum craftworkers. "There have always been times when we worked together," the local joiner explains, "but this time it came from the top, it was the owners' decision. They wanted a real all-round werkraum job."

The name **werkraum** alludes to a long tradition of initiatives committed to high quality in craftwork and design: Germany's united Handcraft Workshops and Craft Leagues of the 1900 period, and the craft workshop education supported by the Bauhaus around 1920, all followed on from principles pioneered by William Morris and John Ruskin back in the 1860s.

Das Alte muss untergehen, damit Neues entstehen kann. Den Gästezimmern wird mit brachialer Gewalt zu Leibe gerückt.

Old things must perish so that new things may be born. Here, muscle is being put into demolishing the old bedrooms.

Das reaktivierte Stübchen mit dem nach dem Umbau verschwundenen seitlichen Eingang. Das Kreischen der Motorsäge macht den Weg frei für das feine Klappern von Besteck und das leise Klirren edler Gläser. Gepflegtes Tafeln.

The resurrected Stübchen (small restaurant) without the side entrance – now dispensed with. The screech of the power saw fades into the past, succeeded by the faint rattle of cutlery and the clink of fine glassware. Elegant dining.

Tischlermeister Wolfgang Dorner (links) und Zimmerer Hermann Nenning im bewegten Diskurs. Die Abstimmung der Handwerksarbeiten – im konkreten Fall: Fenster und Wände – geschieht meist direkt vor Ort. Mit dem für den Fenstermacher typischen 1:1 Entwurf auf einem Stück Holz.

Master joiner Wolfgang Dorner (l.) and carpenter Hermann Nenning in animated discussion. Ensuring a perfect interface between different craft trades – in this instance windows and walls – is usually handled on the job. And with the aid of the window-builder's usual drawing – actual size and on a plank.

Hermann Bechter, Installateur: der Mann, der die Krone im Kopf hat. Ein Genie; sein Blick geht durch Wände und noch im größten Chaos erkennt er eine Ordnung. Sein Werk verschwindet hinter Rigips und Täfer: und ist so präsent wie kaum ein anderes.

Hermann Bechter, master plumber – the man with the entire Krone in his head. A genius! He can see through walls, and in the direst chaos he perceives order. His work has to vanish behind Rigips plaster and wooden panelling. But it is omnipresent in a way that few other trades can rival.

Zimmer 312: Mit Zabin und Fingerspitzengefühl geht es dem alten Baubestand an den Kragen, bzw. an die unter 1960er-Jahre-Verkleidungen zum Vorschein kommende noble Stuckdecke (die wartet heute in der Werkstatt des Stukkateurs auf ihr weiteres Schicksal).

Room 312. It takes a demolition hook and skilful fingers to get to grips with the building's historic structure, here the superb stucco ceiling emerging behind the false ceilings installed during the 1960s. (For the time being it is in the plasterer's shop awaiting the next turn in its fortunes.)

54 Tonnen einer speziellen Betonmischung sorgen in den neuen Zimmern für Halt und Ruhe. Die 170 Jahre alten Balken der Krone tragen's mit Gelassenheit.

A special concrete mix – 54 tons of it – has been laid in the new rooms, to give added stability and ensure quiet. For the 170-year-old beams of the Krone, it's not a problem.

Das bloßgelegte Strickwerk im Bereich der neuen Zimmer: Wir sind wieder soweit wie unsere Vorgänger anno 1838, und der Einbau der neuen Fenster kann beginnen.

Exposed "knitwork" of timbers adjacent to the new rooms. We are at the stage our predecessors reached in 1838, and installation of the new windows can begin.

Werkstätten

Der eigentliche Innenausbau kommt aus den Werkstätten von zwei Handvoll werkraum-Mitgliedern, davon alleine die Hälfte Holzverarbeiter im engeren Sinn – entsprechend der hochentwickelten und am Ort sogar für die Gäste aufbereiteten Holzkultur. Dabei ist weniger der Umfang der Aufgabe der Grund für diese Vielzahl, sondern die unterschiedlichen Stärken und Fähigkeiten der einzelnen Werkstätten: „Wie unter Brüdern ist die Arbeit aufgeteilt worden, wo gefragt wird: Was kannst Du am besten, was Du…", ergänzt der Tischler.

Holzkultur ist in und um den Ort in allen Facetten mit eigenen Augen und zu Fuß zu erleben auf einem eigens angelegten Weg, vorgestellt in dem Büchlein „Holz Kultur Hittisau".

Die eine Werkstatt etwa erinnert mit den großen Apparaten der CNC-Fräsen und den Feinräumen für Lackarbeiten fast schon an eine Fabrik. Was diese Werkstatt verlässt, ist von maschineller Perfektion, widersteht starker Beanspruchung und glänzt makellos. Die neuen Einbauten der Bäder kommen hierher – Glanz der neuen Möbel.

Die andere Werksatt werkt mit einer der fortschrittlichsten Zimmereien unter gemeinsamem Dach – Holzhausbau auf höchstem technologischen Niveau gründend auf tradiertem Wissen über den Hausbau, ausgesprochene Tüftler mit langer Erfahrung in der Sanierung typischer Bregenzerwälder Häuser. „Da lernt man, was es braucht: Schauen, hinterfragen, auf den Grund gehen, dann erst entscheiden," weiß der hiesige Meister. So gedeiht das Gespür für Räume – die Vertäferung der neuen Gaststuben, die Bänke, die sie zusammenbinden, sowie die Türfutter, Übergang von Raum zu Raum, kommen aus dieser Werkstatt.

Zur Wand gehören die Fenster mit Läden, die aus einer ortsansässigen, auf Fenster spezialisierten Schreinerei kommen, wo den Festlegungen durch heutige Maschinen hier eine Fase und dort eine Nut abgerungen wird, was das Werk der seit langem gepflegten regionalen Kultur feingliedrigen Fensterbaus ebenbürtig macht.

Craft workshops

The actual interior furnishings come from the workshops of two small groups of werkraum members, fully half of the workers concerned being woodworkers in the strict sense. This reflects the locality's highly developed wood culture, which is even featured in the profile offered to visitors. That so many workers took part was not due to the size of the task, but to the differences in individual workshops' particular strengths and specialisms. The joiner explains: "It's like dividing jobs up between brothers, you're asking: 'What can you do? And what about you…?'"

One of the workshops, for example, with its massive CNC lathes and its clean-rooms for varnishing, is reminiscent of a factory. Every item made in this shop is of machine-tool perfection, extremely robust, and gleams immaculately. This is where the new bathroom furnishings come from – with the high gloss of brand-new furniture.

The next workshop is under the same roof as one of the most progressive carpenters' businesses – timber-built housing using advanced technology and founded on proven traditional housebuilding knowhow;real sticklers for detail, with long experience in the renovation and modernisation of typical Bregenzerwald buildings. "That's where you learn it all: have a good look, get the story, investigate properly – and only then decide what to do," advises the master craftsman. That is how one picks up a feeling for rooms. The panelling of the new public rooms, the benches holding it together, and the jamb linings, connecting the rooms, come from this workshop.

The wall includes the windows and their shutters. These come from a joinery business based in the village, window specialists, where modern machines set the dimensions but craftsmen chamfer an edge here and add a rabbet there, so that the work produced matches up to the old and cherished regional culture of light and graceful window structures.

Wood culture in all its aspects is there to be seen and experienced first-hand and on foot, in the village and in the countryside nearby, following a specially designed trail described in the "Holz Kultur Hittisau" booklet.

Wieder eine andere Werkstatt gleicht einem Loft: Die intensive Auseinandersetzung mit tradierter Bregenzerwälder Einrichtung – Stühle, Kommode und Kredenz etwa – zeigt sich in den vielen Musterstücken. Von hier kommen die Gebrauchsmöbel: Frühstücksbuffets, Teeschränke, Servicecontainer.

Schließlich die Werkstatt, deren größtes – nicht nur räumliches – Volumen ein riesiges Holzlager ist. Hier ist zuerst das Holz selbst das Thema: Es wird teilweise selbst angebaut, ist auf jeden Fall mit Forstleuten handverlesen, wird zum rechten Zeitpunkt geschlagen, hat die Zeit, mehrere Jahre bei Wind und Wetter und anschließend unter Dach zu lagern und zu trocknen, was die folgende Verarbeitung erst ermöglicht, die immer unter Ausnutzung der Materialeigenschaften geschieht, etwa wenn Volumenänderungen infolge Feuchte und Temperatur gesteuert beim Fügen genutzt werden. Das Werkstück wird möglichst als Ganzes verarbeitet, Hilfsmittel minimiert, was den Anteil an Handarbeit erhöhen mag, doch der Haltbarkeit zugute kommt. Das Tun dieser Werkstatt wird von der Frage getrieben: Was ist dem Stoff angemessen? Und entsprechend: was der Aufgabe, was dem Wirtshaus, was dem Gast? Es ist nicht übertrieben: Hier ist das Gewissen des Baues. Und es nimmt nicht Wunder, dass, was dem Leib des Gastes am Nächsten ist, von hier kommt: Stühle, Sessel, Betten, Möbel des Schlafraumes.

Doch halt! Von Fall zu Fall vermittelt zwischen solchem Holz pur und dem Gast die Ebene, die den Sinnen schmeichelt – Polster, Stoffe, Leder. Der „leichte" Sinn des Einschmeichelns kommt aus der Polsterwerkstatt – nichts Leichtes freilich, sondern gelegentlich mit viel Kraft in Form gebracht, gekonnt, geübt und erfahren wie alles gute Handwerk.

Hierher gehören ebenfalls die Oberflächen der Wände. Wo nicht genau unterschiedene und auf den Bedarf abgestimmte Hölzer wirken – von der weichen Haut der sägerauen Weißtanne bis zur robusten Glätte gehobelter Fichte –, sind sie das Werk des Malers: das fein marmorierte Weiß von Decke und Wänden; das tiefe, farbige Glühen der in vielen Schichten aufgebauten Spachteltechnik der Bäder – in keinem Fall reicht ein einmaliger Auftrag. Und wo die Farbe dem Lauf des Wassers nicht widersteht, wechselt die Wand zum Stein, dessen Glitzern und Glimmen zur Vorfreude auf das Sprühen und Glitzern des Wassers unter dem indirekten Licht wird.

Was Auge und Fingerspitzen am fernsten scheint, worauf aber alles steht: der Boden, auch er – in Anlehnung an die alte Gaststube oder als Bestandteil der neuen Raumkomposition der Gästezimmer – meisterlich in Holz gefügt.

Hochgebildetes Bauhandwerk und der Aufschwung der Landwirtschaft brachten im frühen 19. Jhr. eine Raum- und Möbelkultur hervor, die in Stuhl und Kanapee gipfelt, einst in jeder Stube als Einzelstück zu finden.

A third workshop resembles a loft. Intensive study of traditional Bregenzerwald furnishing styles – in such things as chairs, chests-of-drawers, sideboards – has clearly gone into the numerous pieces on show. It was from here that the domestic items were sourced – breakfast bars, tea cupboards, crockery cupboards.

And finally, the workshop in which the largest volume – not just spatially – is a vast wood-store. Here the focus is primarily on wood as such. They grow some of it themselves, always selecting individually with the forester on hand, fell at just the right time, weather it outside for several years before bringing it in for storing and drying. It takes all that to prepare the wood for subsequent processing, which always takes advantages of wood's physical properties as a material: for instance, changes in volume induced by humidity and temperature can be exploited when parts are being dovetailed together. As far as possible the piece is handled whole, and there is minimal use of aids – which adds to the work to be done by hand, but improves durability. In this shop, work is always done with certain priorities in mind. First: what is right for this material? Then: and what is right for the job in hand, for the hotel, for the hotel guest? It is no exaggeration to claim that here we are seeing furniture-making's conscience. And it is no surprise to find that it is the items most immediate to the guest's bodily comfort that are made here: upright chairs, easy chairs, beds, bedroom furniture.

No, hang on a minute! Sometimes the plain wood and the guest do not meet directly but enjoy the mediation of an intervening layer with sensory appeal – upholstery, textiles, leather. This flattery of the senses is planned for and engineered in the upholstery shop, though at that stage subtlety is not enough: moulding may take considerable force, and skill, practice and experience matter as in all good craftwork.

It is here, too, that the wall surfaces originate. Where effects are not from different woods, finely demarcated and each suited to purpose – from soft-skinned, rough-finish silver fir to the hard smoothness of planed spruce – they are the work of the painter: the finely marbled white of ceiling and walls; the deep, rich glow of the palette knife's multi-layered work in the bathrooms. Nowhere is a single coat sufficient. And in places where paint would not stand up to running water, walls are in stone, glistening and sparkling in the indirect lighting like a happy anticipation of cascading, glistening water drops.

The furnishing furthest from the eye and the fingertips, but on which ultimately all rests, is the floor. And the floor too, whether it follows the style of the old Stube or is a design element in the modern statement of the guest bedrooms, is masterly woodwork by experts in wood.

Sophisticated construction and joinery skills and agricultural prosperity in the early 19th century led to a culture of interior design and furniture-making, its finest products including the chair and sofa once found as single items in every front room.

Was die einen zum Schlafen bringen soll, ist für die anderen Anlaß zu höchster Wachsamkeit. In der Holzwerkstatt von Markus Faißt wird das Bett Odysseus gebaut: Pures Holz in kunstvoller Verzahnung.

It's designed to lull people to sleep, and yet from this craftsman it demands the utmost vigilance. We are in the woodworking shop of Markus Faißt, where the "Odysseus" bed is under construction: all wood, and beautifully dovetailed.

Worauf wir sitzen? Worauf wir schauen? Eckbänke, Wand- und Deckentäfer (im Stüble) aus der Tischlerei Michael Kaufmann in Reuthe/Bezau.

What do we sit on, and what, seated, do we see? Corner benches, and panelling for walls and ceiling (in the Stüble), from Michael Kaufmann's furniture-making workshop in Reuthe/Bezau.

Wovon wir essen? Wovon wir uns bedienen? Buffetmöbel und Tische von der Tischlerei Anton Mohr in Andelsbuch.

What do we eat from? Where is our food laid out? Buffet pieces and tables from Anton Mohr's furniture-making workshop in Andelsbuch.

Worauf wir uns betten? Was uns umgibt? Worauf wir sitzen? Woran wir arbeiten? Betten, Stühle, Täferwand und Verbauten in den Zimmern: Holzwerkstatt Markus Faißt in Hittisau.

What cossets us as we sleep? What's all round us? What do we sit on? And work at? Beds, chairs, wall-panelling and facings in the bedrooms, from the Markus Faißt woodworking shop in Hittisau.

Wie weich wir sitzen? Wie bequem es ist? Bestimmt der Polsterer: Mohr Polster, Johannes Mohr in Andelsbuch.

How soft the seat? How comfortable? – It is the upholsterer who decides. Mohr upholstery – Johannes Mohr, Andelsbuch.

Wie cool der Wein lagert? Wie beständig die Schrift? Wie exklusiv das Metall? Schmiedearbeiten: Josef Eberle in Hittisau.

How cool can a wine cooler be? Will the labels stay on? How fine the metal? Artist blacksmithing by Josef Eberle, Hittisau.

Ob wir immer schön auf dem Boden bleiben? Parkettböden vom Fussbodenprofi: Josef Fröwis in Bezau.

Beauty where'er you walk? – Exquisite parquet floors by the flooring expert – Josef Fröwis of Bezau.

Isch des nü? Sind Zimmermänner Feinspitze? Holzbau und Täferwände (neu!) im Gang erledigt Zimmerei Nenning in Hittisau.

Is it new? Are carpenters the absolute tops for precision? Corridor woodwork and panelled walls (new!) were put in by Nenning Carpenters, Hittisau.

Wer geht gern baden? Ist Platz im Kasten? Bädermöbel und Kästen aus der Tischlerei Rüscher in Schnepfau.

Oh, the joys of a hot bath! Is the cupboard roomy? Bathroom fittings and cupboards by Rüscher Joinery, Schepfau.

Wer kann sich das alles ausmalen? Malerarbeiten Martin Lässer und Michael Fetz aus Alberschwende.

Need a painter's imagination? – Paintwork by Martin Lässer and Michael Fetz, Alberschwende.

Stein und Wasser wie Bruder und Schwester. Natursteinverkleidungen in den Bädern von Steinmetz Lenz Alberschwende.

Stone and water in perfect harmony. Natural stone facings in the bathrooms by Lenz Stonemasons, Alberschwende.

Was führt die Krone im Schilde?
Wirtshausschild restauriert von Jürgen Raid in Krumbach.

Signs of the times.
Inn sign restored by Jürgen Raid, Krumbach.

Worauf wir stehen? Mehr Durchblick! Teppiche und Vorhänge: Anton Wüstner in Mellau.

What turns us on? More perspective please! Carpets and curtains by Anton Wüstner, Mellau.

Streng und Locker

Angesichts von Umfang der Aufgabe, Zahl der Gewerke und Betriebe, Höhe der Erwartung will das Staunen gar nicht vergehen: Wie geht das alles zusammen? Eigentlich sind das drei Fragen – mindestens.

Zuerst sind da die Bauherren, der Entschluss, die Wahl des Architekten. Nicht ohne Erfahrung, fiel die Entscheidung wohlüberlegt zugunsten eines jungen Bewerbers aus der Nachbarschaft, der sich – selbständig seit einem halben Jahrzehnt – mit preisgekröntem Wohnungsbau und Wettbewerbserfolgen im kommunalen Bauen einen Namen gemacht hat. Sicher haben aber die persönliche Bekanntschaft und die Gewissheit, Engagement und Aufmerksamkeit zu finden, den Ausschlag gegeben. Was wohl richtig war: Deutlich über dem Üblichen lagen die Stunden, die für die Planungsgespräche aufgewandt wurden. Dabei hat jeder, der beteiligt ist, Anspruch auf Gehör – nicht im Sinn eines Konsens, sondern „Bedürfnisse gut äußern, definieren können, was soll ein Ding können, dann erst diskutieren", so der Architekt. Dass Nutzer, Betreiber, insbesondere die Hausherrin ein gewichtiges Wort – „im Hotel muss alles kundenfreundlich sein, da muss auch der Architekt manche Kanten abschleifen" – mitreden, versteht sich. Doch ebenso beteiligt sind Handwerker, bringen die Erfahrung ihres Gewerks, aber auch die aus vergleichbaren Fällen mit, sind anfangs, als es um die Richtung geht, gemeinsam dabei, später, soweit es ihren Part betrifft. So ist jeder über alles im Bild, und weiß, was gerade von ihm erwartet wird. Der Planungsprozess ist eher der Entfaltung einer Idee vergleichbar als einer exekutierten Hierarchie einsamer Entschlüsse. Die Handwerker schätzen, dass der Architekt sie fragt, bevor er zu seinen Lösungen kommt, und sie wissen, dass die richtige Lösung mitunter erst auf der Baustelle gelingt, „live" geschieht, auch mal mehr Zeit braucht. Das alles beeinträchtigt seine Autorität keineswegs, wird doch im Gegenteil erkennbar, wo seine Belange liegen. Beides wird ihm abverlangt: Entschlüsse in Rückkopplungen und streng lineare Entscheidungen – „Ein solches Projekt muss ich laufen lassen und dann muss ich kontrollieren". So bekommt der Architekt das Projekt in den Griff, was sich dann in einer großen Zahl Zeichnungen niederschlägt, darunter auffallend viele Innenraum-Abwicklungen von hoher Anschaulichkeit.

In den Griff bekommen – das ist eigentlich, was Handwerk ausmacht. Im Wechselspiel von Vorstellung und Sinnlichkeit, von Kopf und Hand entfaltet sich eine handwerklich gemachte Sache. Das Handhaben des Stoffs steuert den Gedankenflug.

Dass die **Hand** im Handwerk nicht nachgeordnetes Organ, sondern Ausführungs-, Sinnes- und Erkenntnisorgan ist, weiß, wer dem Schreiner bei der Arbeit zusieht. Für Kant ist die Hand das Fenster des Geistes, für Aristoteles das erste Werkzeug, für die moderne Hirnforschung ist sie neuronal vernetzt und der Neurologe F. Wilson misst der tätigen Hand eine Schlüsselrolle bei der Menschwerdung zu.

Strict yet easy-going

Given the scale of the project, the number of teams and businesses involved, and the level of expectation, one has to ask: how on earth is this all to gel together? In fact there are three questions there. At least three!

First of all, you have the clients, the decision, the choice of architect. With past experience a factor, the choice fell after due consideration on a young applicant from the local area. He has had his own practice for half a decade, and has made a name for himself with an award for residential design and competition wins in communal building. But it will have been knowing him personally that made the difference, one could be certain the commitment and the active interest would be there. And there I guess we were right: the planning discussions went on appreciably longer than average. Everyone involved has a right to be heard. It's not that there has to be a consensus, but – as the architect puts it: "Spell out clearly what is required, be able to define what you want a thing to do for you, and only then talk it over." Obviously there has to be significant input from the end users and the management, in particular the lady running the house – "In a hotel everything has to be the way the customer likes it, and that means the architect sanding off a lot of rough edges." However, the workforce are also very much involved, bringing the experience of their various trades, as well as what they have picked up from similar jobs. At the start, when it is more general issues, they contribute collectively, but later on, in the more specialised questions, they bring in their own particular perspective. So everyone is wholly in the picture and everyone knows what he or she is expected to contribute. The planning process is more like the growth of an idea, it's not really a hierarchy implementing individual decisions handed down from the top. Workmen appreciate the architect asking their views before reaching his solutions, and they know that the right answer may come up actually on site, "live," so to speak – or may take time to find. None of this diminishes the architect's authority; in fact it indicates what he thinks important. He has both to supply feedback on decisions taken and also to take strictly linear decisions – "I have to let a project like this take its course, and then assess the position." In this way the architect gets a grip on the project; a lot of drawings result, including a strikingly large number of well-visualised variants for the interior design.

Getting a grip on it – that is what craftwork is all about. It's the dialectic of ideas and sensory experience, of head and hand, that produces genuinely crafted things. Physically handling the material guides the flow of ideas.

The **hand** is not an "extremity" when it comes to handcraft, but an organ with executive, sensory and learning functions – as will be realised by anyone who watches a joiner at work. For Kant, the hand was the mind's window; for Aristotle, the first tool; in modern brain research, it is part of the neuronal network, and the neurologist Frank R. Wilson credits the activity of the hand with a key role in the process by which we became human.

Vertraut und neu

Auch im Hinblick auf die Sache selbst, den Bau, fragt sich, wie all das zusammengeht. Seit seiner Errichtung vor 170 Jahren wurde in dem Haus dasselbe Handwerk betrieben, Gastgewerbe mit Küche und Unterkunft. Man kann dem Haus ansehen, dass es ursprünglich höheren Zwecken gewidmet war, doch ließ es sich bestens seiner wirklichen Bestimmung anpassen. In seiner Bauart unterscheidet es sich nicht von irgendeinem der zeitgleich errichteten Bregenzerwälder Bauernpaläste – so heißen die stattlichen Höfe dieser Zeit.

Auf gemauertem Sockel erheben sich 3 Stockwerke in Holzmassivbauweise, Blockbau bzw. Strickbau von ca 15 cm Wandstärke. Maßgebend für den Grundriss ist die Stube – das Schmuckstück des Bauernhauses: Links und rechts eines zum Platz hin führenden zentralen Flurs mit einläufiger Treppe liegen solche Räume von ca. sechs mal sechs Meter, einst wohl alle stattlich ausgestattet. Noch bietet einer das Bild, wie es zur Zeit der Entstehung darin ausgesehen hat: großzügig belichtet über je zwei Fenster an der Außenwand, die die räumliche Gliederung auf den ersten Blick enthüllen, die sich in der Gliederung der getäferten Wand in feinerem Maßstab fortsetzt und die mit der ebenso geteilten Decke nicht zu Ende ist. Wände, Decke, die umlaufende Eckbank, der Boden, die Möbel: alles aus Holz gefertigt, je nach Bedarf von unterschiedlicher Art und Verarbeitung, doch durch die Feinheit der Gliederung verbunden. Ausschlaggebend war damals in vielerlei Hinsicht die Anforderung der Konstruktion (Abmessung des Baustoffes, Wärmeschutz, Winddichte, Sauberkeit), doch immer wird diese in der Durchbildung verfeinert, auch mal bis zum Schmuck getrieben, so dass ein Raum entsteht, dessen Zauber vom Stoff, Maß und Verhältnissen lebt. Es wird an der Herkunft von der Stube liegen, dass dieser Raum sich mit seinem Wechsel von Nähe und Abstand, von Intimität und Geselligkeit bestens für eine Gaststube eignet. Der Betrieb rechtfertigt diese Raumbildung. So darf man die Bregenzerwälder Raumkunst als eine solche bezeichnen, die bei der Funktion ihren Ausgang nimmt, wenn, mit Goethe, Funktion „Dasein als Tätigkeit" meint.

Die **Stube** ist der Beitrag der Alpen zur Wohnkultur: ein beheizter, rauchfreier Raum. Im Bregenzerwald bewirken weite Fenster, silbrig schimmernde Wandverkleidung, regelmäßige, doch nie gleiche Einrichtung, was bereits um 1830 der Reiseschriftsteller L. Steub pries: „Stattliche Häuslichkeit, reinlich, sparsam, licht, reizend…"

The familiar and the new

The task itself, the actual rebuilding project, poses the same question: how is this all going to come together? Ever since the house was first built 170 years ago, the same business has been carried on within its walls: the hospitality trade, providing meals and accommodation. One can see the building was originally intended for higher purposes, but it adapted excellently to what has been its actual destiny. Structurally it is no different from any of the imposing farmhouses dating from the same period and known as the Bregenzerwald peasant palaces.

Its 3 storeys, on a masonry pedestal, are of blockhouse (or "knitted") solid wood construction, with outer walls about 15 cm thick. The ground plan is essentially drawn up round the Stube – in the farmhouse, always a show room. A central hallway giving on the square outside, with a single flight of steps, is flanked to left and right by rooms of this type, each about six metres square, and all presumably at one time handsomely furnished. One still presents the appearance it had in the very early days: generously lit by two windows in each outer wall; they at once show up the room's spatial organisation, and it in turn continues on a finer scale in the articulation of the wall panelling and does not even end with the similarly structured ceiling. Walls, ceiling, the corner bench following the walls, the floor, the furniture – all this is made of wood, different types of wood and differently finished according to function, but all harmonised by the fineness of the articulation. In many ways, what mattered in those times was the constructional requirements (dimensions of building materials, heat insulation, anti-draught protection, hygiene), but refinement was always introduced in the detail and might even be taken to the length of ornament, so that all in all the charm of the finished room was a matter of materials, dimensions and proportions. Its origins in the Stube explain why this room with its balance of closeness and distance, of intimacy and social function, is admirably suited as a hotel Gaststube. The catering business justifies this room design. On this basis one may describe the art of room design in the Bregenzerwald as art based on function, taking "function" here in Goethe's sense of "existence as activity".

The **Stube** is the Alps' contribution to the culture of living: a heated but smoke-free room. In the Bregenzerwald it is given added appeal by wide windows, the silvery sheen of the wall cladding, and broadly consistent – yet never uniform – furnishings. The combination won praise from a very early travel writer, L. Steub, in about 1830: "Dignified domesticity, clean and tidy, frugal, well lit, charming…"

Es sind diese Eigenschaften, die auch zum Maß für die neu zu gestaltenden Gaststuben wurden. Einige waren in der Nachkriegszeit modernisiert worden, wobei die Demonstration, dass man es auch größer kann, der Gastlichkeit nicht gut bekommen ist. Nicht um Stil, sondern um Belebung der bekannten Raumqualitäten musste es jetzt gehen. Die neuen Räume zeigen, dass dies nicht Kopie, sondern Variation, Umformung, Abwandlung des angeschlagenen Themas heißen kann, „ein Spiel mit dem, was der Raum vorgibt", so der Architekt.

Also wurde, wo sinnvoll, der Wand/Fenster-Rhythmus in der hauseigenen Proportion wiederhergestellt, die Verhältnismäßigkeit des Raumgefüges durch neue Wandscheiben angedeutet, die Wandverkleidung erneuert, wärmetechnisch verbessert und teils nachgebaut, teils neu interpretiert. So steht dem etwas lässig-fließenden Gefüge des Bestandes eine streng-kantige und umgreifend durchgeführte Ordnung gegenüber. Bei allen Möbeln, von der fest eingebauten umlaufenden Bank über Schränke und Buffets bis zum Stuhl kommen neue, eigene Modelle zum Einsatz, wobei insbesondere der Stuhl Bezüge zum biedermeierlichen Ideal sachlicher Gebräuchlichkeit erkennen lässt. Alle neuen Möbel sind aus hartem Rüster (Ulme), die Wand dem Bestand entsprechend Fichte oder Tanne. Ein kleines high tech-Meisterwerk hat man sich mit dem Weinschrank geleistet, der auf kleinstem Raum Ausstellung, Kühlung, Umluft, Wärmedämmung, und Beleuchtung integriert. Vom örtlichen Schlosser mit Kälte- und Beleuchtungstechnikern entworfen und konstruiert, zeigt er Schwarzstahl und seine Verarbeitung und belässt die Technik im Verborgenen.

Das gilt auch für die Schlafräume im Obergeschoß, wo vieles, was dem Komfort des Gastes dient, verborgen bleibt: vom Schallschutz (nichts knarzt und knackt in dem immerhin 170 jährigen Bau), über Installation, Heizung und ausgeklügelte Lichtsteuerung. Das Raumgefüge hält sich an die vorgegebene Struktur, die Räume selbst sind vergrößert, die Raumgestaltung entwickelt sich frei und begleitet das Eintauchen in den privaten Bereich. Prägen beim Betreten des Zimmers das lichte Weiß der Wände und die großen Fenster mit den belebten Ausblicken den Eindruck, so wird es um den Schlafbereich mit der Fassung durch flächenbündige Weißtannenpaneele körperhaft-intimer, um in den Bädern mit der warmen Ocker der Wände und dem Naturstein fast leibhaftig nah zu rücken. Die Möbel in massiver Eiche unterstreichen die körperhafte Verlässlichkeit und erlauben sich bei der Fügung gar ein konstruktives Ornament. „Wir zeigen, wie sich es fügt – was schön wird, wenn man es richtig macht", bemerkt der Tischler dazu.

Die Verbindung des Nützlichen mit dem Schönen steht im Zentrum des Biedermeier und bildet, so C. Witt-Döring 2006 in „Wege zur Einfachheit", den „Schlüssel zu dieser trotz seiner Empfindsamkeit so materialistischen Welt."

These qualities became the yardstick for decisions on those public rooms that were to be redesigned. Some of them had been modernised in the immediate postwar period, demonstrating that one could certainly make rooms bigger, but at the expense of their convivial ambiance. What mattered now was not style but recapture of the old atmosphere. As the new rooms show, this is not achieved by copying what went before, but by variation, adaptation, modulation of the given theme, "an improvisation on what the room suggests," as the architect puts it.

And so, where it made sense, the wall-and-window rhythm characterising the building was restored, the proportionality of the room arrangement was hinted at by fitting new wall plates, the wall covering was renovated, given better insulation, and partly restored to look as it had before, partly re-interpreted. As a result, the rather easygoing, fluid arrangement of the old structure now contrasts with an uncompromisingly hard-edged and widely imposed new style. For all the furniture, from the fixed bench round the walls to cupboards and buffet tables to chairs, new models were specially chosen; the chairs in particular are reminiscent of the Biedermeier ideal of practical usefulness. All the new furniture is hard elm, but the walls – in keeping with the original – are spruce or fir. It was decided to invest in a little masterpiece of high tech in the form of the wine cooler which combines display, chilling, ventilation, insulation and lighting in ultra-compact form. Designed and built by the local artist blacksmith with help from refrigeration engineers and electricians, it presents black steel and the workmanship to the world, and keeps its technology to itself.

Much the same is true, too, of the bedrooms upstairs, in which much that ensures the guests' comfort remains unseen – from soundproofing (the building may be 170 years old, but there are no creaks and groans) to plumbing, heating and ingenious lighting controls. The arrangement of the rooms conforms to the pre-existing structure, the rooms themselves are larger, room design is individual and sits easily with the feeling of entering the private domain. The first impressions on entering the room are the clear white of the walls and then the big windows and the life and movement outside; then in the sleep zone the associations are warmer and more intimate, thanks to the surrounding flush-inset panels in silver fir, and finally, in the bathrooms, the warm ochre of the walls and the natural stone suggest closeness almost to the point of touch. The furniture, solid oak, reassures with the dependability of physical objects, and the jointing even rises to a bit of functional ornament. "We show how it fits together – and that looks good when you get it right," comments the joiner.

The combination of the useful and the beautiful is at the heart of Biedermeier, and – according to C. Witt-Döring in his "Wege zur Einfachheit" (Paths to Simplicity) (2006) – is "the key to this mawkish and yet deeply materialistic world of ours."

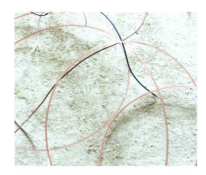

Für sich und gemeinsam

Nochmals die Baustelle: zwei Monate, insgesamt eine Besetzung in der Größe dreier Schulklassen, wie am Schnürchen abgewickelt, eins ins andere greifend – das geht gut, weil sich die Beteiligten als werkraum-Mitglieder längst kennen. Man nennt sich beim Vornamen, kennt Werkstatt und Mitarbeiter, weiß um Stärken wie Schwächen. Dabei kann man gerade an Tagen mit dichter Besetzung feststellen: Jeder schafft für sich, geht andern aus dem Weg, macht Platz, mancher zieht gar das Wochenende vor, der Bodenleger verweigert sich schlicht, wenn noch irgendwer da ist. Doch wenn Not am Mann ist, ist jeder zur Stelle, hilft der Zimmerer selbstverständlich dem Schreiner aus, hat das hinweisende Nachfragen des Installateurs manchen Konflikt im Vorfeld ausgeräumt, hat sich ausgezahlt, dass der Trockenbauer auf jedes Maß besteht, wäre ohne das gegenseitige Drängen der schönste Terminplan Papier geblieben. Der vereinbarte Standard erfordert den Blick voraus und zur Seite: „Ma denkt ja weiter", sagt der Trockenbauer, denn ohne bereits bei der Unterkonstruktion darauf Rücksicht zu nehmen, gelingt später die Oberfläche und das Zusammenspiel mit anderen Gewerken nicht. Unvorhersehbares – Maßabweichungen beim Einbau der neuen Fenster etwa – wird gewerkübergreifend vor Ort erörtert und gelöst, wenn es sein muss auch ohne Bauleitung.

On one's own and together

Back to the building works: two months now, a total crew equal in numbers to three classes of schoolchildren, everything running like clockwork, dovetailing nicely. It's going well because the people concerned, being werkraum members, have known each other for years. They are on Christian name terms, know who works in which shop and with which mates, know each other's strengths and weaknesses. All the same, especially on days with more than usual on site, one can see that everyone is working on his own account, keeping out of others' way, giving them room; some actually prefer to work at weekends, and the floor layer simply refuses to work until everyone has gone. And yet, and yet: when the chips are down, people always rally round, the carpenter naturally helps the joiner out, a pointed question from the plumber has pre-empted many a later dispute, it has paid off that the erector rigorously checks every measurement, and without the mutual nagging no doubt even the best work schedule would have meant nothing. The work standard agreed on makes it vital to look ahead and watch the flanks at the same time: "You have to think ahead," says the erector, because if you don't think about it while you're at the foundation level you can be sure that it will go wrong higher up and you will be out of synch with the other trades. When the unforeseen happens – finding the new windows don't fit when you put them in, for instance – the problem is discussed among the various trades there and then and sorted out, if necessary without the site engineer being present.

„Zuerst muss ich mit der Arbeit selber zufrieden sein, dann der Kunde", so beschreibt der Polsterer seinen und des werkraum Anspruch, und wer weiß, dass neben ihm und nach ihm mit dieser Einstellung gearbeitet wird, gibt sich keine Blöße, schaut besonders genau hin, erlaubt sich freilich auch mal einen Hinweis gegenüber dem Nachbarn. Das kann er, weil er – und ist er noch so sehr Fachmann – eine Vorstellung vom Ganzen hat. Rivalität verträgt sich hier mit Respekt. Die Vielzahl der Verantwortlichen führt nicht zu Einebnung, sondern spornt an. Wenn das Wort Bauhütte eine Berechtigung hat, dann hier, wo das Zusammenwirken Energien freisetzt, wo das Ganze mehr als seine Teile ist – wo jeder für sich schafft und alle gemeinsam und beides zusammen. Dies steht in deutlichem Kontrast zu andersartigen Erfahrungen, die immer häufiger geboten werden: industrielles Bauen der neuesten Art. Ein geschlossenes System aus ausgefeilten Produkten, umfänglichem Vorgespräch, Empfehlung hauseigener System-Lösungen, Massenermittlung und CAD-Planung im firmeneigenen Büro, abgestimmt auf die Abnahme durch die Behörde, Rechnungsstellung und – ja, zwischendurch Montage durch den örtlichen Handwerker. Und stellt der Bauherr dann fest, dass Art und Umfang gar nicht so gewünscht waren, so lernt er, dass die Rückabwicklung erheblich mehr holpert als die geschmierte Projektabwicklung.

Beide Verfahren können bildhaft gegenübergestellt werden: Letzteres gleicht dem Fertiggericht für die Mikrowelle: schnelles und risikoloses Deponieren eines vorgefertigten Gerichts in einem abgestimmten Gerät unter Ausführung einer Anweisung – Abwicklung eines fremd erstellten Musters, eine Tautologie. Das handwerkliche Bauen gleicht dem gebräuchlichen Kochen: Stoff, Energie und Wissen entfalten sich im Austausch und Wechsel.

Man kann verstehen, dass die Wirtsleute ihr Glück im Handwerk des werkraum gesucht haben. So führen Bau und Baustelle vor, was Architektur ist: Raumbildung durch Herstellen von Beziehungen. Im vorliegenden Fall: in jeder Hinsicht geglückt.

First to be satisfied with the work has to be me, then the customer," says the upholsterer; this amounts to a statement of his own credo and that of the werkraum. If I am aware that those alongside me and coming after me have that attitude to their work, then I will not let them catch me out, I will really watch my step, though I might sometimes drop a hint to my neigbour. And I can do that, however much of a specialist I am, because I also have an overview, I can see the project as a whole. There is rivalry here, but also mutual respect. Lots of people have responsibility here – but it doesn't discourage initiative, it actually becomes a challenge. If the idea of a builders' fraternity means anything, it's what we have here. The way we work together releases energies that make the whole more than the sum of the parts, that have every individual working for himself and for everyone else, both at the same time. This is a big contrast with what you now get more and more often – mass-production building of the latest type. It's a closed system: clever products, wide-ranging negotiations before the start, firm pushes its own system solutions, quantity surveying and CAD planning in the company offices, all with an eye to planning permissions, then invoicing and – yes, of course, at some point a local craftsman on site to put it all together. And if the client then realises that it's too big or too small or not what he wanted, he's going to find out unpicking it is a lot slower and harder than the greased lightning project delivery was.

So you can have industrialised building, or you can use craftsmen. I see it like this. If you go for high-powered industrial methods, it's like putting your freezer meal into the microwave. Pre-fabricated stuff, bung it into the right machine – quick, easy, risk-free – and follow the instructions. You're just following somebody else's template. Now try putting craftsmen on your building job. Suddenly you're back to traditional cooking. You are combining materials with energy with knowhow. And that mixture works.

All in all, one can see why the Krone proprietors put their faith in the craft skills of the werkraum group. As a result, the rebuild and the work site demonstrate what architecture means – the creation of spaces by establishing relationships. The outcome in this instance is a success in every respect.

„Alles was überhaupt gedacht werden kann, kann klar gedacht werden. Alles was sich aussprechen lässt, lässt sich klar aussprechen." (Ludwig Wittgenstein)

"Anything that can be thought at all can be thought clearly. Anything that can be expressed at all can be expressed clearly." (Ludwig Wittgenstein)

„Der Gedanke enthält die Möglichkeit der Sachlage, die er denkt. Was denkbar ist, ist auch möglich." (Ludwig Wittgenstein) Quod erat demonstrandum. Tischler und Fenstermacher in der fertigen Stube.

"The thought contains the possibility of the state of affairs which it thinks. What is thinkable is also possible." (Ludwig Wittgenstein) Quod erat demonstrandum. Joiner and window furnisher in the finished Stube.

Renate Breuss

Kochen und Bauen
Cooks too are builders

Im Raum des Werkens und Bauens entstehen nicht nur Häuser, Möbel und Einbauten, auch Speisen werden gebaut. Der Ort der Speisenherstellung ist die Küche, das Baumaterial sind die Rohstoffe, ausgewählt, bearbeitet und zusammengesetzt von den Köchen und Köchinnen.

Baustelle Küche

In der Kronenküche sind mit Wilma und Helene zwei Meisterinnen am Werk.
Tag für Tag bilden sie aus einzelnen Zutaten ein neues Ganzes und tragen es auf
in Form von Suppen und Sulzen, Ragouts und Braten, Crèmes und Kuchen.
Die Küche ist ein Ort der Transformation und der ständigen Veränderungen –
die Küche ist täglich neu eine Baustelle.

Thema: Sulz
Baumaterial:
Kalbskopf, Kalbsfüße, Essig, Salz, Gelbe Rüben, Zwiebeln
Prozesse:
mechanische (häuten, schälen, schneiden, zerpflücken), thermische (sieden),
physikalische (gelieren)
Werkzeuge:
Hände, Messer, Beil, Löffel, Seiher
Künstlich begrenzte Räume:
Kochtopf, Schüssel

Cutting, trimming and shaping, then assembly is what creates houses, furniture and fitments – but also the meals we eat. Cooks too are builders. The site is the kitchen, and the building materials are the raw foods that are selected, prepared, and then assembled or combined by the cooks.

The kitchen as building site

In the Gasthof Krone's kitchen, Wilma and Helene are two master craftswomen at work. Every day they take individual ingredients and create a new entity, which they serve up in the form of soups and stews, meat in aspic or oven-roasted, bavarois and gateaux. The kitchen is a place of transformations and constant metamorphosis – a new building site daily.

Theme: Veal in aspic
Building materials:
Calf's head, calf's feet, vinegar, salt, carrots, onions
Processes:
mechanical (skinning, peeling, slicing, flaking), thermic (boiling), physical (jellifying)
Tools:
hands, knives, chopper, spoons, sieve
Artificially restricted spaces:
Saucepan, bowl

Handwerker zu Tisch

Auf dem Wochenplan der Umbauphase stehen Krautspätzle, Bratwürste mit Kartoffelsalat, Schweineschopfbraten, Kaiserfleisch mit Sauerkraut, Kartoffelsuppe, Penne mit Gorganzola, Spaghetti mit Tomatensauce, Wurstnudeln, Tiroler Gröstl oder besonders beliebt bei den Süßlern ein Griesauflauf mit Apfelmus, ein Kaiserschmarren mit Apfelkompott.

Krautspätzle – wie sie Handwerker gerne mögen

Spätzle
500 g griffiges Mehl
Salz, Muskatnuss
5 Eier
Milch
½ kg Sauerkraut, gekocht
5 Scheiben fetter Bauchspeck in Würfel geschnitten
Kümmel ganz, Pfeffer
(Für 4 Personen)

Für die Spätzle Mehl, Eier, Muskatnuss, Salz mit Milch zu einem „schlampigen" Teig mischen.
Durch ein Spätzlesieb in kochendes Salzwasser drücken und aufkochen lassen. In kaltem Wasser abschrecken. Den würfelig geschnittenen Speck anbraten, Sauerkraut dazugeben. Die Spätzle daruntermischen und knusprig braten. Mit Kümmel und frischem Pfeffer abschmecken. Dazu schmeckt am besten Blattsalat!

Der Gasthof bleibt während der Umbauarbeiten geschlossen, die Küche ist in Betrieb. Gekocht wird nicht nur für die eigene Familie, auch für die Handwerker ist Platz am Mittagstisch. Diese in der Mitte des Tages liegende Mahlzeit, sozusagen umgeben von der Arbeit, hat ihren eigenen Stellenwert. Das aufgetragene Essen verkörpert dieselbe Arbeit und Wertschätzung wie die ihre, es stillt den Appetit und es macht zufrieden. Die Verpflegung von im Hause tätigen Arbeitern und Handwerkern ist eine kaum mehr gelebte Tradition. Neben der Sättigung schafft sie Beziehung und Verbundenheit. Essen prägt sich ein im Gedächtnis, ist Brücke zu einem Ort, zu einem Menschen, zu einem bestimmten Geruch, zu einer großzügigen oder geizigen, sinnenfreudigen oder puritanischen Geschichte. Die grüne Erbse auf dem Riesenteller hat in diesem Umfeld nichts verloren. Schnickschnack ist der Handwerker Sache nicht. Gewissheit bleibt vielmehr ein Teller voll sämiger Kartoffelsuppe oder die kecke Konsistenz einer schönen Scheibe Kaiserfleisch im Sauerkraut. Das ehrt die Köchinnen, dafür gebührt ihnen Dank.

Craftworkers' lunch

During the rebuild period, a week's menus feature spaetzle with sauerkraut, grilled sausages with potato salad, roast neck of pork, Kaiserfleisch (smoked loin of pork) with sauerkraut, potato soup, penne with gorgonzola cheese, spaghetti with tomato sauce, noodle and sausage bake, Tiroler Gröstl (cold meat pieces with sautéed potatoes or pasta), or – for the sweet tooth – semolina pudding with stewed apples, or Kaiserschmarren (pancake pieces with raisins) and apple compote.

The hotel and restaurant are closed during the rebuilding, but the kitchen is operational. Apart from the cooking needed for the owners' family, there are places at lunch for all the building workers. This meal taken in the middle of the day – surrounded by work, as it were – has a special meaning. The food served represents the same work and the same respect as theirs, it satisfies the appetite and brings contentment. Once widespread, the tradition of providing a meal for labourers and craftsmen employed on the premises has almost died out. Apart from keeping people fed and content, it is good for relationships and bonding. Food is remembered later, it is a bridge linking one in memory to a place, another person, a particular smell, a past experience of generosity or meanness, sensual delight or puritanical restraint. This lunch-table is not the place to dish up a stick of celery on a huge plate: craftworkers don't go for arty food. What they can be sure of here is more like a plateful of thick creamy potato soup, or the perky texture of a fine slab of Kaiserfleisch (smoked pork) in a heap of sauerkraut. Such dishes do credit to the ladies who have cooked them. They deserve their thanks.

Spaetzle with sauerkraut – the way the workers like it

For the spaetzle:
500 g durum wheat flour
salt, nutmeg
5 eggs
milk
500 g cooked sauerkraut
5 slices fat belly pork, diced
whole caraway, pepper
(Serves 4)

Make the spaetzle by blending the flour and eggs with salt, nutmeg and the milk to make a fairly soft dough. Press through a spaetzle sieve into boiling water. Bring back to the boil. Refresh with cold water. Brown the diced pork in a pan, add the sauerkraut. Mix in the spaetzle and cook till crisp. Add caraway and fresh ground pepper to taste. Best side-dish is a green salad.

Tischler, Kühltechniker, Installateur, Bauherr usw. am Mittagstisch: Konzentriertes Zuhören und sachkundiges Referieren statt protzigem Einander-Übertrumpfen. Alle angetrieben vom selben Hunger nach Perfektion und Krautspätzle!

Joiner, refrigeration engineer, plumber, client and others at the lunch table. Focused listening, and explanation from knowledge – not rivalry and oneupmanship. All spurred on by the same hunger for perfection and (of course) spaetzle with sauerkraut.

Rohstoff Landschaft

Die Speisen porträtieren das Bild einer essbaren Landschaft, vom Bodensee bis nach Balderschwang, von Krumbach bis nach Sibratsgfäll. Auf den Tisch kommen frische und natürliche Produkte – die Vermählung von Bach, Flur und Wald, in flüssiger und fester Form.

Tischler und Zimmerer kennen ihre Hölzer gut. Sie wissen um das ideale Fassaden-, Schrank- oder Täferholz, vom materialgerechten Einsatz der Weißtannen, Birnen und Fichten, von besseren und schlechteren Standorten, vom richtigen Schlagen und Lagern. Genauso wissen die Köchinnen Bescheid um die Eigenschaften und Qualitäten ihrer Rohstoffe und deren Bearbeitung. Wenn eine Landschaft zum Schmecken gebracht wird, sprechen die Ressourcen und der Umgang mit diesen Ressourcen immer mit. Aus den umliegenden Fluren, Bächen, Alpen und Wäldern beziehen die Köchinnen das, was die Region hergibt: frische Forellen aus der Subersach, Zander und Felchen aus dem nahen Bodensee, Lamm und Kalb vom benachbarten Bauern, Wild vom heimischen Jäger. Der Käse kommt von den Alpen und von den örtlichen Sennereien. Je nach Senn und Alpe kann die geschulte Zunge feinste Nuancen und Unterschiede erkennen. Was an Rohmaterialien und Zutaten gebraucht und nicht erhältlich ist, wird andernorts zugekauft, so wie die Holzverarbeiter nicht ihren ganzen Bedarf in den örtlichen Wäldern abdecken. Gerne würde man mehr Gemüse aus der Region beziehen, doch Gemüse wird zu wenig angebaut, dasselbe gilt für das Rindfleisch. Als Reaktion auf einen Markt, der mit den Ansprüchen und Vorstellungen der beiden Köchinnen nicht mithalten kann, werden neuerdings auch das Gedeckbrot und das Schwarzbrot wieder selbst gebacken.

Grüner Bohnensalat mit Thymian, Hittisauer Frischkäsle und gerösteten Sonnenblumenkernen – nach unserer Art

½ kg grüne Bohnen, gekocht
1 Schalotte
Saft von ¼ Zitrone
Olivenöl
Sherryessig
Salz, Pfeffer
frischer Thymian
2 Frischkäsle
Sonnenblumenkerne
etwas Butter
(Für 4 Personen)

Alle Zutaten für den Salat mischen. Die Frischkäsle in Würfel schneiden und um den Salat anrichten. Mit den in Butter gerösteten Sonnenblumenkernen bestreuen.

Raw materials: countryside

The dishes conjure up a vision of a gastronomic landscape, from Lake Constance to Balderschwang, from Krumbach to Sibratsgfäll. The products brought to the table are fresh and natural, a marriage of river and field and forest, to be consummated as food an drink.

Joiners and carpenters know the various types of wood well. They know the best woods for exteriors, for cupboards, for panelling. They know just how to work with silver fir, pearwood, spruce, about the best and the lesser locations, about proper felling and seasoning. In exactly the same way, our cooks understand the nature and characteristics of their raw materials and the methods of preparing them. When the countryside is made to taste good, the natural resources and the way they are handled are part of the experience. The cooks draw on what the region has to offer, from its fields and rivers, its alps and forests: fresh trout from the Subersach brook, pike-perch and felchen (whitefish) from nearby Lake Constance, lamb and veal from neigbouring farmers, game from local hunters. The cheese comes from the high pastures (the "alps") and from local dairies. The experienced cheese-lover can detect the subtlest nuances and variations in cheeses from different dairies or mountainsides. Any raw materials or other ingredients needed but not available locally are bought elsewhere, in the same way as the wood turners have to look beyond the local forests for some of the species needed. We would love to source more vegetables locally – but there are just not enough grown locally. The same applies to beef. For one necessity in particular, the market cannot provide all that our cooks want to offer, and so they have come up with their own response: they have now gone back to baking their own table bread and schwarzbrot.

Green bean salad with thyme, very young and delicate Hittisau cheese and roasted sunflower seeds – Gasthof Krone style

500 g cooked runner beans or French beans
1 shallot
juice of ¼ lemon
olive oil
sherry vinegar
salt and pepper
fresh thyme
2 rounds of cheese
sunflower seeds
a little butter
(Serves 4)

Mix all the salad ingredients. Cut the cheeses into small pieces and arrange round the salad. Roast the sunflower seeds in butter and sprinkle over.

… Werkstatt für ursprüngliche Nahrungsmittel und Landschaftspflege, sowie Tourismusmotor in einem.

… All rolled into one, a workshop for natural fresh foods and for landscape conservation – and a major tourist attraction as well.

Familiäre Prägung

In der Krone nehmen die Vorfahren, unauffällig und diskret, neben den Jüngeren Platz. Zu den begehrten Klassikern gehören zeitaufwändige Schmorgerichte genauso wie kurz gebratene Fisch- und Fleischstücke.

Dem Ort ihrer Herkunft verbunden zu bleiben, schließt den Blick über den Tellerrand hinaus nicht aus. Beide Köchinnen sind in Gasthäusern groß geworden, haben gelernt bei ihren Müttern und Schwiegermüttern. Ohne Nostalgie wird das stundenlange Rüsten für die handgemachten Pommes Frites erinnert, werden schulfreie Wochenenden mit Küche konnotiert. Kochen gehörte von Kind an dazu, ohne gleich an eine spätere Profession zu denken. Das gute Essen war und ist wichtig für die ganze Familie, es hält, wie der Volksmund sagt, Leib und Seele zusammen.

Neben der familiären Prägung bilden eine praxisnahe schulische Ausbildung, Reisen und Lesen die solide Basis für die heutige Kronenküche. Ungarische Wochen, Kräutergnocchi und Crème brûlée sind Referenzen an so gewonnene Eindrücke, aufgebaut und immer wieder aufgefrischt über viele Jahre. Leichtfertig passiert die Aufnahme einer neuen Speise in die Speisekarte jedenfalls nicht. Doch mit der Zeit steht man grundsätzlich auf gutem Fuß. Alles was Zeit und Muße braucht, langsam und bedächtig herangart, innig durchdrungen von der Hitze und den Zutaten ist, überzeugt unter dem Stichwort Schmoren. Rindsgulasch, Kalbszüngle und Schweinsbäckle, Burgunderbraten und klare Fleischsuppen, „dieses Essen tut einem einfach gut", sagt die Seniorchefin. Selbstbewusst behaupten diese Gerichte ihren angestammten Platz auf der Speisekarte, neben einem zartes Fenchelcarpaccio oder einer gebrannten Joghurtcrème.

Die treuen Stammgäste hat man sich mit Verlässlichkeit und Sorgfalt erobert. Von der Kontinuität des Hauses sind auch die Gourmetkritiker überzeugt. Seit 13 Jahren ist die Krone ein prämiertes Haubenlokal.

Bodensee-Felchenfilet mit frischen Kräutern.
Ein Kronenklassiker – so wie es sich gehört

8 Felchenfilets
Salz
Zitronensaft
Petersilie, Schnittlauch, Kerbel, Dill
Butter
(Für 4 Personen)

Die Filets mit Salz und Zitronensaft würzen und in der heissen Pfanne beidseitig braten. Alle Kräuter fein schneiden und auf den Filets verteilen. Mit nussbrauner (!!) Butter übergiessen. Schmeckt gut mit Salzkartoffeln oder Risotto!

A family thing

In the Gasthof Krone, discreetly and without fuss, older generations are present at table alongside the young. Classic dishes always in demand at the Krone range from time-consuming slow-cooked casseroles to quick-fried fresh fish and steaks.

Remaining closely involved with your home town does not mean you never look beyond your backyard. The two ladies who cook for the Krone grew up in hotels themselves and learnt from their mothers and mothers-in-law. They look back – dry-eyed – at the hours of preparation that went into the home-made French fries, and the weekends on which school holidays simply meant kitchen duty. From childhood onwards, cooking was a part of their life, not that they thought of it then as a profession to take up later on. Good food was and is important to everyone in the family – in the words of the old saying, it keeps body and soul together.

Early experience in family cooking was followed by practice-oriented school lessons, travel and reading as solid all-round preparation for their role in the Krone of today. Hungarian Weeks, herb gnocchi and crème brûlée are reminders of one-time new experiences that have been built on and refreshed time and again over many years. It is certainly no easy matter for a new dish to win a place on the Krone menu. But time and our lady chefs have a good relationship. Every dish that requires time and patience, that needs to be slowly and carefully cooked to perfection, permeated through and through by the heat and the flavours, promises its quality in the word schmoren, to braise or casserole. Beef goulash, veal tongue, pork cheek, Burgundy roast, consommés – "Food like this quite simply does you good," says the head chef. These dishes effortlessly retain their long-established places on the menu, rubbing shoulders with a delicate fennel carpaccio or a yoghurt crème brûlée.

The Krone's faithful regulars have been won over by utter dependability and by taking trouble. The continuity of its performance is attested by the food critics: the Krone has been a starred, award-winning gourmet restaurant for the last 13 years.

Lake Constance felchen fillet with fresh herbs – A Gasthof Krone classic comme il faut

8 fillets of felchen
salt
lemon juice
parsley, chives, chervil, dill
butter
(Serves 4)

Season the fillets with salt and lemon juice and fry on both sides in a hot pan. Chop all the herbs finely and sprinkle over the fillets. Having melted and browned (NB!) the butter, pour it on top. Excellent with boiled potatoes or risotto!

Ästhetik der Sparsamkeit

Der Anfang wird in der Krone noch gerne mit der Suppe gemacht. Klare Fleischsuppen stimmen ein auf das Kommende. Das Felchenfilet wird schon seit 20 Jahren so zubereitet, wie es sich gehört. Weil es so wie es ist, frisch aus dem Bodensee, kurz im Butter gebraten, perfekt ist. Klar, bekömmlich und ohne Attitüden.

Gebrannte Joghurtcreme – eine Crème brulée auf Wälderisch

380 ml Sahne
50 g Zucker
5 Dotter
Schale von ½ Zitrone
Mark von ½ Vanilleschote
140 g Naturjoghurt
brauner Zucker zum Bestreuen
(Für 4 Personen)

Backofen auf 90 Grad vorheizen. Sahne aufkochen, mit Zucker, Zitronenschale, Vanillemark und Joghurt verrühren. Mischung kurz aufkochen, vom Herd nehmen und langsam unter die Dotter rühren. Creme unter ständigem Rühren auf ca. 75 Grad erwärmen. Durch ein Sieb passieren und in 4 Schälchen oder Suppenteller füllen. Die Creme für ca. 2 h im Rohr stocken lassen. Dann für mindestens 4 h kalt stellen. Vor dem Servieren die Crème mit braunem Zucker bestreuen und mit einem Bunsenbrenner caramelisieren. Dazu passt am bestens Marillenröster!

Ein ausgeprägter Sinn für Ökonomie prägt nicht nur das Bauen und das Handwerk. Im Gasthof Krone hält man vom Rundumkochen – gemeint sind Garnituren und Dekorationen – nicht viel. In der Verbindung von Schönem mit Nützlichem zählt, was schmeckt, in klarer und sauberer Note. Die goldbraune Kruste eines Brathuhns ist gleichermaßen schön und gut, der Rosmarinzweig ist Geschmacks- und Farbgeber in einem. Der Ausdruckswert einer Speise wird in ihr selbst gesehen, hervorgebracht über die Technik der Zubereitung und die Stimmigkeit von Gewürzen. Vom weit verbreiteten Trend des Überdekorierens lässt man sich nicht aus dem Konzept bringen. Die 10jährige Zusammenarbeit von Mutter und Tochter basiert auf klarer Planung und Arbeitsteilung. Fleisch und Fisch sind das Metier der Älteren, Suppen und Süßes obliegen der Jüngeren. Die Zusammensetzung von Teigen und Crèmes folgt festgelegten Proportionen und Verhältnissen. Diese sind auf Karteikarten für die Nachwelt in knapper Form festgehalten. Was mit Worten nicht zu sagen ist, das muss probiert und erfahren werden: die richtige Konsistenz einer Kuchenmasse, die Leichtigkeit einer Eiercrème, das gleichmäßige Aufgehen eines Brot- oder Hefeteigs. Einigkeit herrscht darüber, dass die alten Rezepte noch immer die besten Vorlagen für Kuchen und Konfekt bereithalten. Das Sortiment der Weihnachtskekse ist auf 10 erprobte Sorten beschränkt. Nicht mehr, aber auch nicht weniger.

Für die Kronenküche bezeichnend ist eine Form der Zurückhaltung, die im Auge behält, was machbar und bekömmlich ist. Der eigenen Vorstellung Genüge zu tun, kann dabei ein hoher Anspruch sein.

Good taste and restraint

At the Krone, we still like to start with soup. A fine consommé sets the tone for what is to come. For 20 years past, the fillet of felchen has been prepared for our guests in exactly the way we prepare it today – simply because done this way it is perfect, fresh-caught in Lake Constance and fried quickly in butter. Straightforward, good for you, and no airs and graces.

It is by no means only in construction and craftwork that commonsense attitudes to spending prevail. At the Gasthof Krone, we are not fans of artwork cuisine – meaning dishes bedecked with garnishes and decorations. When it comes to combining beauty and usefulness, what counts is the taste, and that needs to be clear and clean. The crisp gold crust on a roast chicken is appealing visually – and delicious; a sprig of rosemary gives both colour and flavour. The "statement" made by a dish is contained in the food itself, brought out by the method of preparation and the harmony of the seasonings. We don't feel the need here to follow the widespread fad for elaborate decoration. The mother-and-daughter team at the Krone have enjoyed ten years of successful cooperation, thanks to clear-headed planning, and division of labour. Meat and fish are the province of the older chef, soups and sweets are looked after by her daughter. The recipes used for the various pastry types or for egg custards (for example) always retain the same well-proven balance and proportions. And they have been preserved in summary form in a card-index for the benefit of future generations. There are things that cannot be explained in words, but have to be tried out and learned by experience – such as the right consistency for a particular cake-mix, the lightness of an egg custard, or how to get a bread or cake dough to rise evenly. We are unanimous that the old recipes still give the best basic mixes for cakes and biscuits. Our range of Christmas biscuits has 10 well-tried varieties only. No more than that, but not fewer either.

The mark of the Krone style of cuisine is its characteristic restraint: it keeps the focus on straightforward food that people find agrees with them. But living up to what we ourselves expect can be demanding.

*Yoghurt crème brûlée –
A crème brûlée in
Bregenzerwald style*

380 ml cream
50 g sugar
5 egg yolks
zest of ½ lemon
flesh of ½ vanilla pod
140 g natural yoghur
tbrown sugar for sprinkling on
(Serves 4)

Pre-heat the oven to 90 C. Bring the cream to boil, stir in sugar, lemon zest, vanilla and yoghurt. Bring the mixture back to the boil for a moment, remove from heat and gradually mix it into the egg yolks. Stirring continuously, warm the mix to about 75 C. Sieve and pour into 4 ramekins or soup bowls. Leave the crème in the warm oven for about 2 hours. Then chill for at least 4 hours. Before serving, sprinkle with brown sugar and caramelise with a blowtorch. The nicest accompaniment is apricot purée!

Peter Natter

Der Gast in der Krone

The guest experience at the Krone

„Rast! Gast sein einmal. Nicht immer selbst seine Wünsche bewirten mit kärglicher Kost. Nicht immer feindlich nach allem fassen, einmal sich alles geschehen lassen und wissen: was geschieht, ist gut."

Immer wieder sind es diese wunderbaren Worte des vielleicht sinnlichsten aller Dichter, Rainer Maria Rilke, deren ich mich – als Gast! – beim Anblick der Krone wie von selbst erinnere. Ob in frostklammen klaren Winternächten, wenn das Licht aus den Stuben warm auf den Dorfplatz leuchtet, oder an flimmernd heißen Sommernachmittagen auf der Terrasse sitzend, wenn die Welt still zu stehen scheint: die Krone erfüllt Rilkes Worte mit Leben. Und sie erfüllt den Gast mit Leben, mit einer stillen, behäbigen Gelassenheit, mit einer fast schon verloren geglaubten Sorglosigkeit.

"Rest! Guest for the moment, not always appeasing my wishes with eked-out supplies. Not always aggressively hunting and grabbing, just once letting things happen to me – and knowing what happens is good."

Again and again, it is the haunting German original of these words, by Rainer Maria Rilke, perhaps the most sensuous poet of them all, that comes back to me unbidden when I come in sight of the Krone at the start of another visit. Be it on clear icy winter nights with the light from the Stuben spilling its warmth across the village square, or on shimmering, baking summer afternoons when I sit on the terrace and the world comes to a standstill: the Krone brings Rilke's words to real life. And it fills the guest with new life, with a quiet and leisurely serenity, a peace of mind that one had almost lost hope of finding again.

Nun ist manches neu geworden in und an der Krone. Neu geworden? Lieber würde ich einfach sagen: wieder geworden! Gemäß dem „Werde, der Du bist!", das uns die Philosophen zurufen. Nicht nur, dass die Fassade ihr früheres Gesicht (bis auf den in alten Fotografien noch präsenten äußeren Stiegenaufgang in den ersten Stock – aber irgendwann ist der Zug der Zeit eben abgefahren!) und der Eingang ein helles, einladendes, verführerisch-kokettes Holzkleid erhalten haben. Der Umbau der Krone hat ein beglückendes Ineinander von Alt und Neu bewirkt. Die neuen Gaststuben: die nach dem Erbauer benannte Bechter-Stube und das daran anschließende Stüble, sind mit Ausnahme der Decke nigelnagelneu. Und doch verspürt der Gast in ihnen ein Aufgehobensein, wie es nur sehr große Vertrautheit gewährt. Kein Wunder: diese Räume verdanken ihre Atmosphäre und ihren Charakter Jahrhunderte alter Handwerkskunst, dem Respekt des Bauherrn vor der Substanz des Hauses (im materiellen und im metaphysischen Sinne!) und dem tief in der Tradition verankerten Gefühl, sowie der Innovationsfreudigkeit der beteiligten Handwerksbetriebe. Natürlich ist in der Krone (fast) nichts mehr so wie zur Zeit der Erbauung vor 170 Jahren und auch nur wenig so wie vor 50, 60 Jahren: Aber alles in der Krone ist so, wie es alle immer wollen hätten können: und vor allem: wie es den heutigen Gast in die von Rilke so treffend beschriebene selige Stimmung versetzt.

Das Neue in der Krone erzählt eine alte, eine uralte Geschichte so, dass auch wir Heutigen sie verstehen: und sie als unsere eigene erkennen und lieben lernen. Nicht zuletzt eine Geschichte von der Sehnsucht nach Ankommen, nach Geborgenheit, nach gastlicher Wärme. Die sechs neu erbauten Gast-Zimmer, die sogenannten „Werkraumzimmer", erzählen diese Geschichte besonders eindringlich. So ist es weit mehr als nur ein nostalgisierender Gag, wenn der Gast die Zimmer durch die schönen alten Türen betritt: Tatsächlich sind diese Zimmer eine bewusste, faszinierende und im besten Sinn zeitgemäße Neuinterpretation der alten Mythen von Herkunft, Heimat, und Handwerk. Die Materialien: Holz, Stein, Stoff verweisen auf längst Bekanntes. Die Form, die ihnen hier gegeben wird, hebt sie aus der Zeit heraus und schafft somit einen magischen Raum, an dem sich die Bewohnerin, der Bewohner unwillkürlich neu erfahren. Nichts, aber schon gar nichts, ist hier prätentiöser Selbstzweck; alles ist durch und durch wälderisch: Selbstbewußt (mit einer kleinen, entschuldbaren Neigung zum Stolz), gediegen, natürlich, geradlinig. Eleganz verbindet sich mit Behaglichkeit, Praktisches mit Verspieltem, Wertvolles mit Coolness. Das Neue in der Krone muss nicht so tun, als ob es alt wäre, es spielt uns nichts vor: Es lebt ebenso im Alten, wie das Alte in ihm. Und von allem natürlich nur das Beste.

And now much has been made new at the Krone. Made new? I think I prefer to say simply: Restored! Just as the philosophers advise: "Become what you are!" It is not merely that the front façade has been restored to its earlier appearance (with the exception of the outside steps up to the first floor, as shown in old photographs – but some things really did get borne away with that ever-rolling stream!) and the entrance treated to a bright, appealing, coquettish, almost seductive timber fronting. It's more than that. The rebuild of the Krone has brought about a very pleasing fusion of old and new. Except for their ceilings, the new public rooms – that is, the Bechter-Stube (named after the founder) and the adjoining Stüble – are absolutely brand-new. And yet in these rooms the hotel guest has that sense of safe and homely ensconcement that a place can give as a rule only with long familiarity. And it is no wonder, for these rooms owe their atmosphere and their character to a craftsmanship honed over centuries, to the respect felt by the owners for the building's substance (in the physical and metaphysical senses!) and the emotion tied up with long traditions, and to the natural innovativeness of the craft shops involved in the project. Obviously, (almost) nothing in the Krone is just the way it was when the place was new 170 years ago, and not much is as it was even 50 or 60 years back. However, everything in the Krone is the way that everyone might well have always wanted it to be. And above all: everything is as it needs to be in order to put the present-day guest in the seraphic mood so aptly described in Rilke's verse.

What is new at the Krone tells an old – a very old – story in such a way that we moderns can understand it, and can learn to recognise it as our own and to love it. Not least, it is a story of the yearning to arrive, to find refuge, to feel the warmth of hospitality. This tale is told particularly vividly by the six newly built guest bedrooms, those referred to as the werkraum rooms. It is far more than just a gimmick, a nostalgic harking-back, when a guest opens the lovely old doors to enter the rooms: these rooms truly are a conscious, fascinating – and in the best sense contemporary – reinterpretation of the old myths of origin, homeland and handicraft. The materials – wood, stone, cloth – point back into prehistory. The form they have been given here lifts them out of time and thus generates a magic around them that causes the person entering the rooms to encounter himself or herself anew. Nothing, absolutely nothing here, is pretentious and pointless; everything is wälderisch (local to the region) through and through; everything is sure of its place (with a slight, pardonable tinge of pride), solid, natural, clean of line. Elegance embraces comfort, practicality learns to be playful, serious worth does not preclude looking cool. What is new at the Krone has no need to pretend to be old. It is not trying to fool us: it lives in the old, just as the old lives on in what is new. And of all things, obviously, only the best.

Wer als Gast in die Krone kommt, ist mehr als König: Er ist er selbst. Poetischer ausgedrückt: Er (sie!) erwacht in einen wundervollen Traum hinein. Kann man schönere Worte finden als die von Rilke, um sich nach einem gemütlichen Abend oder einem längeren Aufenthalt von der Krone zu verabschieden? – „Aus dunklem Wein und tausend Rosen rinnt die Stunde rauschend in den Traum der Nacht." …

Every guest arriving at the Krone is more than king for a day: here one can be oneself. To put it poetically – once in the Krone, he (or she) wakes from life outside into a wonderful dream. And when the time comes to leave the Krone again – after two hours or two weeks – can there be any more beautiful words to come to mind than those of Rilke? – "From dark, bubbling wine and a thousand roses the hour flows out into night's dream." [Rilke quotation translated by C. Fitz Gibbon: Copyright © C. Fitz Gibbon 1973]

Der neue Weinschrank zieht die Blicke auf sich, ein magisches Wunderwerk, das Technikfreaks ebenso ins Schwärmen bringt wie Weinfreunde. Schön ist was nützt!

The new wine cooler is a real eye-catcher, a magic and marvellous chest, rated really, really cool by wine-lovers, of course – and by techno geeks!
There is beauty in usefulness...

Die Bechter Stube: Ein Gesamtkunstwerk; edel, hell und genial: Praktische Forderungen (Unterbringung des Frühstücksbuffets für Hausgäste) und ästhetische Vorgaben in geglückter Harmonie.
Wälderstube goes cosmopolitan.

The Bechter Stube – a gesamtkunstwerk, fusion of all the arts – effortless, light-filled, superb. Practicality (the residents' breakfast buffet is here) and aesthetics in perfect harmony.
The Wälderstube goes cosmopolitan.

Peter Fink (werkraum-Vizeobmann), Bernardo Bader (Architekt), Helene und Dietmar Nussbaumer (Bauherrin und Bauherr): Denn das Ganze ist mehr als die Summe seiner Teile. Wollen und Denken und Tun oder Machen und Herstellen und Handeln: Indem er das seine und sie das ihre tut, entsteht aus dem Plan das Werk. Die Idee der einen ist Realität aller geworden.

Peter Fink (werkraum deputy director), Bernardo Bader (architect) as well as Helene and Dietmar Nussbaumer (clients): because the total equals more than the sum of its parts. Wanting and thinking and doing or making and creating and acting: Whilst he does his and she does hers, the plan evolves into creation. The idea of one turns into reality for all.

Die Mitwirkenden

Architekt **Architect**
DI Bernardo Bader
A-6850 Dornbirn
+43 (0)5572 207896
www.bernardobader.com

Statik **Statics**
DI Ingo Gehrer
A-6973 Höchst
+43 (0)5578 72093 0

Bauleitung **Construction management**
Der Baufuchs – Robert Feuerstein
A-6861 Alberschwende
+43 (0)664 1453223
www.der-baufuchs.com

Baueinrüstung **Scaffolding**
Pfeiffer Gerüstbau
A-6923 Lauterach
+43 (0)5574 75745
www.pfeiffergeruestbau.at

Baumeister **Master builder**
Moosbrugger Bau
A-6866 Andelsbuch
+43 (0)5512 2316 0
www.moosbrugger-bau.at

Beschattung **Blinds**
Manfred Immler
A-6866 Andelsbuch
+43 (0)5512 4869

Beschriftungen **Designations**
Huber
A-6850 Dornbirn
+43 (0)5572 3766
www.hubergmbh.com

RM Design
A-6951 Lingenau
+43 (0)5513 415960
www.rm-design.at

Brandmeldeanlage **Fire detectors**
Siemens
A-6900 Bregenz
+43 (0)51707 68243
www.siemens.com

Elektroinstallationen **Electrical installation**
Elektro Österle
A-6952 Hittisau
+43 (0)5513 6565
www.elektrooesterle.at

Entsorgung **Disposal**
Ennemoser
A-6881 Mellau
+43 (0)5518 2274

Fliesenleger **Tiler**
Fliesen Jams
A-6943 Riefensberg
+43 (0)5513 8809

Fluchtwegleuchten **Escape route lighting**
Zumtobel Lighting
A-6850 Dornbirn
+43 (0)5572 390 167
www.zumtobel.com

Gartenbau **Garden/Landscaping**
Raid Gartenbau
A-6942 Krumbach
+43 (0)664 3216071
www.raid-gartenbau.at

Glaswände **Glass walls**
Glas Marte
A-6900 Bregenz
+43 (0)5574 6722 0
www.glasmarte.at

Heizung/Sanitär
Heating & sanitary installations
Walter Fink
A-6858 Schwarzach
+43 (0)5572 58215

Hifi Anlagen **Hi-fi equipment**
Neha Hifi
D-88171 Weiler im Allgäu
+49 (0)8387 3663
www.neha.de

Kühltechnik **Refrigeration**
Axima Kältetechnik
A-6923 Lauterach
+43 (0)5574 6705
www.axima.info

Lampen **Light furnishings**
Licht & Form
A-6850 Dornbirn
+43 (0)5572 394021
www.lichtundform.at

The participants

Lüftung **Ventilation**
Dietrich Luft+Klima
A-6923 Lauterach
Tel: +43 (0)5574 73797
www.luft-klima.com

Malerarbeiten **Paint work**
Fetzcolor ⓦ
A-6861 Alberschwende
+43 (0)5579 4319
www.fetzcolor.at

Martin Lässer
A-6861 Alberschwende
Tel: +43 (0)5579 3404

Jürgen Raid ⓦ
A-6942 Krumbach
Tel: +43 (0)5513 8227

Naturstein **Natural stone**
Lenz Steinmetz ⓦ
A-6861 Alberschwende
+43 (0)5579 4308
www.lenz-stein.at

Parkettböden **Parquet flooring**
Fröwis Fussbodenprofi ⓦ
A-6870 Bezau
+43 (0)5514 3409

Polsterarbeiten **Upholstery**
Mohr Polster ⓦ
A-6866 Andelsbuch
Tel: +43 (0)5512 3210
www.mohrpolster.at

Schindeln **Shingles**
Moosbrugger Schindeln
A-6934 Sulzberg
+43 (0)5516 2887
www.moosbrugger-schindeln.at

Schlüsseldienst **Key fitting**
Schlüssel Klien
A-6850 Dornbirn
+43 (0)5572 23043

Schmiedearbeiten **Blacksmithing**
Eberle Metall exclusiv ⓦ
A-6952 Hittisau
Tel: +43 (0)5513 2159
www.eberle-metall.at

Walter Feuerstein
A-6952 Hittisau
+43 (0)5513 2268

Spenglerei/Dachdeckerei
Plumbing/roofing
Spenglerei Wild
A-6952 Hittisau
+43 (0)5513 2818

Stukkatur **Plastering**
Otto Manser
A-6870 Bezau
+43 (0)5514 3253
www.manserverputz.at

Teppiche **Carpets**
Anton Wüstner ⓦ
A-6881 Mellau
Tel: +43 (0)5518 2211

Tischlerarbeiten **Cabinet works**
Tischlerei Wolfgang Dorner
A-6952 Hittisau
Tel: +43 (0)5513 30415

Holz-Werkstatt Faißt ⓦ
A-6952 Hittisau
+43 (0)5513 6254
www.holz-werkstatt.com

Kaufmann Zimmerei und Tischlerei ⓦ
A-6870 Reuthe
+43 (0)5514 2209
www.kaufmannzimmerei.at

Tischlerei Mohr ⓦ
A-6866 Andelsbuch
+43 (0)5512 3715
www.tischlereimohr.at

Tischlerei Rüscher ⓦ
A-6882 Schnepfau
+43 (0)5518 2101
www.tischlerei-ruescher.com

Trockenbau **Drywall installation**
Trockenbau Raith
A-6900 Bregenz
+43 (0)664 1234344

Zimmermannsarbeiten **Joinery**
Zimmerei Nenning ⓦ
A-6952 Hittisau
Tel: +43 (0)5513 2874
www.zimmerer-nenning.com

ⓦ werkraum mitglied **werkraum member**

werkraum bregenzerwald

Vereinsgründung	1999
Organisation	über den Vorstand, die Geschäftsstelle und Projektgruppen
Mitglieder	90 vorwiegend kleinstrukturierte Handwerks- und Gewerbebetriebe in den Branchen Holz, Beton, Stein, Metall, Wasser, Stoff, Leder, Licht
Aktivitäten	Ausrichtung Wettbewerb handwerk + form, Ausstellungen, Sonderschauen, Messeauftritte, Gespräche, Vorträge, Firmapräsentationen, Aus- und Weiterbildungsprojekte, Öffentlichkeitsarbeit und Marketing, Betriebs- und branchenübergreifende Kooperationen, Servicestelle und Drehscheibe für Mitglieder
Dokumentation	jährliche Edition einer werkraum zeitung
Ausstellungsraum	werkraum depot in Schwarzenberg
work in progress	Aufbau eines gemeinsamen Ausstellungs-, Kompetenz- und Vermittlungszentrums für Handwerk und Design in Andelsbuch
Geschäftsstelle	werkraum bregenzerwald Impulszentrum Gerbe 1135, A-6863 Egg www.werkraum.at

Gasthof Krone

Hotel	27 Gästezimmer, davon 4 Einzelzimmer, 17 Doppelzimmer (teilweise mit Sitzecke oder separatem Wohnraum), 6 Werkraumzimmer
Restaurant	Ausgezeichnete Küche (1 Haube Gault-Millau, BIB-Michelin), ca. 90 Sitzplätze in drei Stuben, Terrasse mit 24 Sitzplätzen
Ausstattung	Sauna, Garten, Kaminzimmer/Bibliothek, Seminar-, Tagungsmöglichkeiten für ca. 25 Personen
Inhaber	Helene und Dietmar Nussbaumer, Wilma und Herbert Natter
Adresse	Gasthof Krone Am Platz 185, A-6952 Hittisau www.krone-hittisau.at

werkraum bregenzerwald

Association founded	1999
Organisation	Board of Management, Administrative HQ, Project Groups
Membership	90 predominantly small-scale craft and general business enterprises. Trades represented are timber and woodworking, concrete, stone, metal, water, textiles, leather, lighting.
Activities	Organisation of craft /design competitions, exhibitions, special viewings, attendance at trade fairs, networking, talks / lectures, company presentations, training and CPD projects, publicity and marketing, cooperation between companies and between trades, members' service centre and forum
Documentation	werkraum journal, published annually
Exhibition facility	werkraum depot, Schwarzenberg
work in progress	Development at Andelsbuch of a groupwide exhibition facility as well as the establishment of a hub for craft and design
Administration	werkraum bregenzerwald
Impulszentrum
Gerbe 1135, A-6863 Egg, Austria
www.werkraum.at

Gasthof Krone

Hotel	27 bedrooms, comprising 4 single rooms, 17 double rooms (some with lounge area or separate sitting-room), 6 werkraum rooms
Restaurant facilities	Superb cuisine (1 star Gault-Millau, BIB-Michelin). Seating for around 90 in three Stuben, terrace accommodating 24
Facilities	Sauna, garden, chimney-corner room with library, seminar and conference facilities for up to about 25 participants
Proprietors	Helene and Dietmar Nussbaumer, Wilma and Herbert Natter
Contact	Gasthof Krone
Am Platz 185, A-6952 Hittisau, Austria
www.krone-hittisau.at

Schlusswort

Anfangs wurden wir ob unserer Idee, das Handwerk des Bregenzerwaldes in Zusammenarbeit mit dem werkraum in der nunmehr umgesetzten Form in den Mittelpunkt der baulichen Weiterentwicklung unserer Krone zu stellen, für ein bisschen verrückt erklärt, manchmal belächelt, dann wieder beglückwünscht. Die Krone ist und bleibt ein typischer Bregenzerwälder Gasthof. Was in der Zeit von Oktober bis Dezember 2007 baulich verändert wurde, steht für Tradition in frischer, zeitgemäßer Form.

Jetzt ist alles fertig und wir blicken entspannt und zufrieden zurück. Schon vor 170 Jahren haben die Handwerker des Bregenzerwaldes die Krone geprägt: Als während des Umbaus Decken, Wände und Böden offen gelegt waren, standen wir ehrfürchtig vor der Ur-Konstruktion des Hauses.

Am liebsten würden wir morgen schon wieder mit Bauen beginnen, so harmonisch und zielstrebig ging es auf der Baustelle zu und her. Die respektvolle Arbeit neben-, über-, unter- und miteinander war beeindruckend.

Als wir Ende Jänner dann mehr als 90 HandwerkerInnen als Zeichen des Dankes und der Anerkennung bei uns zum Essen begrüßen durften, wurde uns wieder bewusst, wie richtig es war, mit dem werkraum bregenzerwald zu kooperieren, von der im Tal verbliebenen Wertschöpfung gar nicht zu reden.

Helene und Dietmar Nussbaumer

A final reflection

When it became known that we planned, by way of this publication, to show – in co-operation with the werkraum – the Bregenzerwald's craft industries playing a central role in the major rebuilding and modernisation of our Gasthof Krone, we were initially declared to be slightly dotty, and had to endure some pitying smiles; but there were also congratulations. The Krone is a typical Bregenzerwald Gasthof, and will remain one. The changes made by the rebuilding work of the last three months of 2007 represent continuing tradition in fresh, contemporary form.

The work is now finished. Relaxed at last, we look back and are content. It is 170 years since Bregenzerwald craftsmen first gave the Krone building its shape. During the alterations, the old ceilings, walls and floors were exposed. We stood reverently before the building's original skeleton.

We would happily begin work all over again tomorrow – because the multifarious tasks on site were dispatched so harmoniously and purposefully. The mutual respect shown between individuals and others working alongside, above, underneath and with them was deeply impressive.

And then at the end of January, when we had the great pleasure of inviting more than 90 craftsmen and craftswomen to share a meal with us as a mark of our gratitude and admiration, we were again mindful of how right we had been to cooperate with werkraum bregenzerwald, quite apart from any consideration of added value accruing to the local area and community.

Helene and Dietmar Nussbaumer

Die Autoren

Florian Aicher ist freier Architekt in Rotis/Allgäu mit den Schwerpunkten Hochbau und Raumgestaltung sowie deren Theorie und Geschichte. Gastprofessuren führten ihn an die Hochschule für Gestaltung Karlsruhe und die Hochschule der Künste Saar.

Renate Breuß ist promovierte Kunsthistorikerin und Lehrbeauftragte für Kultur & Design an der Fachhochschule Vorarlberg, Studiengang Mediengestaltung. Seit 2001 begleitet sie den werkraum bregenzerwald redaktionell und konzeptuell, seit 2007 im Aufbau eines eigenen Hauses für Handwerk und Design. Seminar- und Vortragstätigkeit zum Thema Kochen, Küche und Kunst mit zahlreichen Veröffentlichungen. Gemeinsam mit Florian Aicher: eigen+sinnig. Der werkraum bregenzerwald als Modell für ein neues Handwerk. München 2005.

Peter Natter (Dr. phil) ist nach langen Lehrjahren im Staatsdienst nunmehr seiner (wahren?) Bestimmung ein schönes Stück näher gekommen. Er tut, was er nicht lassen will, betreibt eine philosophische Praxis, widmet sich dem plaisir du texte, reflektiert und referiert zu Literatur und Philosophie und gibt den garçon d´hôtel in der Hittisauer Krone: „Wir spielen alle, wer es weiß ist klug."

The authors

Florian Aicher is a freelance architect in Rotis/Allgäu focusing on practical, theoretical and historical aspects of structural engineering and (interior) design. He has served as a visiting lecturer at the Hochschule für Gestaltung, Karlsruhe and the Hochschule der Künste, Saar.

Renate Breuß is a graduate art historian and lectures culture & design in media studies at the Fachhochschule Vorarlberg. She's played an active advisory role for the werkraum bregenzerwald since 2001, taking care of editorial and conceptual aspects of the werkraum's activities. Since 2007, she's been busy with the setup of a house specifically dedicated to craft and design. Renate holds seminars and lectures on cooking, cuisine and art and is widely published. Co-author (with Florian Aicher) of: eigen+sinnig. The werkraum bregenzerwald as model for a new craft perspective. Munich 2005.

After a long apprenticeship in the civil service as a teacher, Peter Natter (Dr. phil) today is a good deal closer to his (true?) vocation. He's doing what he can't help doing, runs a philosophy practice, dedicates his time to the plaisir du texte, reflections and lectures on literature and philosophy and acts as garçon d´hôtel at the Krone in Hittisau: "We all play games; the clever ones know this is so."

Sandra Meusburger
Roman Meusburger
Günther Meusburger
Johannes Mohr
Andrea Mohr
Thomas Mohr
Anton Mohr
Elmar Moosbrugger
Wolfgang Moosbrugger
Joe Moosbrugger
Thomas Moosbrugger
Alexander Mori
Angelika Muir-Hartmann
Bernd Nagel
Wilma Natter
Herbert Natter
Peter Natter
Isabella Natter-Spets
Martin Nenning
Hermann Nenning
Jodok Nenning
Manfred Nett
Armin Nußbaumer
Josef Peter Nußbaumer
Franz Josef Nussbaumer
Lina Nussbaumer
Helene Nussbaumer
Dietmar Nussbaumer
Dietmar Oberhauser
Martin Österle
Walter Österle
Antonino Palazzolo
Christoph Paulitsch
Andreas Pech
Erich Pichler
Sandra Pöltl
Jürgen Raid
Gabi Raid
Reinhard Raid
Margit Raid
Werner Raith
Luis Rehm
Martin Reichenberger
Manfred Remm
Franko Rietzler
Beate Rinderer
Martin Ritter
Heinz Rüscher
Nicki Rüscher
Wolfgang Rüscher
Anton Rüscher
Gerhard Rüscher
Fatma Sas
Margret Sattler
Florian Scheuring
Reinhard Schneider
Thomas Schranz
Steffen Schütz
Stefanie Schwarz
Michael Simma
Elias Sinnstein
Harald Sohm
Drazen Spanovic
Caspar Spets
Adrian Springetti
Katharina Steurer
Walter Steurer
Stefan Steurer
Lothar Steurer
Elmar Sutterlüty
Maria Sutterlüty
Stefan Tison
Peter Vögel
Markus Vögel
Alois Vogt
Dietmar Waibel
Simon Wäger
René Wehinger
Katharina Weidinger
Helmut Wiedemann
Reinhold Wild
Daniel Winder
Klaus Winder
Wolfgang Wohlgenannt
Anton Wüstner
Figen Yildiz
Vlado Ziranovic